TO LIE IS HUMAN
NOT GETTING CAUGHT IS DIVINE

Some Other Titles From New Falcon Publications

Undoing Yourself With Energized Meditation
Techniques for Undoing Yourself (CD)
Sex Magic, Tantra & Tarot: The Way of the Secret Lover
Secrets of Western Tantra: The Sexuality of the Middle Path
The Psychopath's Bible
The Black Books
    By Christopher S. Hyatt, Ph.D.
Rebels & Devils: The Psychology of Liberation
    Edited by Christopher S. Hyatt, Ph.D. with contributions by
    Wm. S. Burroughs, Timothy Leary, Robert Anton Wilson et al.
Pacts With the Devil: A Chronicle of Sex, Blasphemy & Liberation
Urban Voodoo: A Beginner's Guide to Afro-Caribbean Magic
Dancing with the Antichrist
    By S. Jason Black and Christopher S. Hyatt, Ph.D.
Taboo: Sex, Religion & Magick
    By Christopher S. Hyatt, Ph.D., Lon Milo DuQuette, et al.
Cosmic Trigger: The Final Secret of the Illuminati
Prometheus Rising
TSOG: The Thing That Ate the Constitution
TSOG: The CD
    By Robert Anton Wilson
Neuropolitique
    By Timothy Leary, Ph.D.
The Chaos Magick Audio CDs
PysberMagick: Advanced Ideas in Chaos Magick
    By Peter J. Carroll
Condensed Chaos: An Introduction to Chaos Magick
Prime Chaos: Adventures in Chaos Magick
    By Phil Hine
The Complete Golden Dawn System of Magic (New, Expanded Edition)
The Golden Dawn Audio CDs
The World of Enochian Magic (CD)
    By Israel Regardie
Beyond Duality: The Art of Transcendence
    By Laurence Galian
Zen Without Zen Masters
    By Camden Benares
Astrology, Aleister & Aeon
    By Charles Kipp

Please visit our website at http://www.newfalcon.com

TO LIE IS HUMAN

NOT GETTING CAUGHT IS DIVINE

by
Christopher S. Hyatt, Ph.D.

Introduced by
Robert Anton Wilson

Illustrated by
S. Jason Black

NEW FALCON PUBLICATIONS
TEMPE, ARIZONA, U.S.A.

International Standard Book Number: 1-56184-199-4
Library of Congress Catalog Card Number: 92-64418

First edition 1992 C.E. (As "The Tree of Lies")
Second Edition 2004 C.E.

Cover Art by Linda Joyce Franks
Interior artwork by S. Jason Black

The paper used in this publication meets the minimum requirements of the American National Standard for Permanence of Paper for Printed Library Materials Z39.48-1984

Address all inquiries to:
NEW FALCON PUBLICATIONS
1739 East Broadway Road #1-277
Tempe, AZ 85282 U.S.A.
(or)
320 East Charleston Blvd. #286-204
Las Vegas, NV 89104 U.S.A.

website: http://www.newfalcon.com
email: info@newfalcon.com

Dedicated Not to the Shepherd

But to The Bearers of Light

—— *Lucifer* ——

And

For Troy Allen Bennett (1968–2004)

One of the Best Men We Had

ACKNOWLEDGMENTS

I wish to thank D.R. Hartmann, John Demmitt, Nicholas Tharcher and S. Jason Black for their valuable ideas, suggestions and editing.

TABLE OF CONTENTS

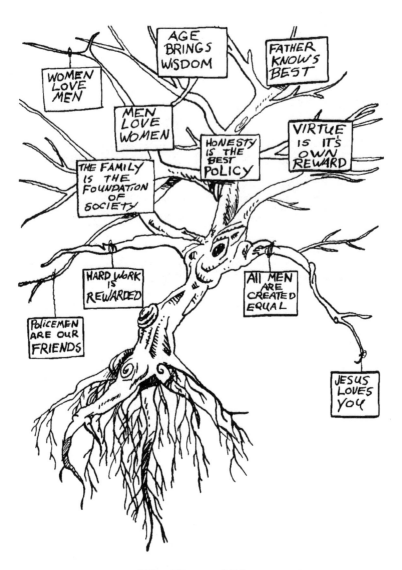

The Tree of Lies

PREFACE

To Lie Is Human,
Not Getting Caught Is Divine.
Learn To Be A Question Mark?

While we desperately yearn for the exotic and wondrous
our first act on meeting it is to turn it into ourselves.
— Hyatt

To have neither great desire nor great despair—
This — this is the goal of all "great" civilizations.
— Hyatt

When the world was made binary
man began to live in paradox.
With paradox came the priest,
the politician and the psychologist.
These three thieves of the soul
became the maker and solver of riddles,
making the poet and artist seem profound.
— Hyatt

Before this binary world—
the fearful was also sacred,
now the fearful is only fearful.
— Hyatt

You use names for things as though
they rigidly, persistently endured;
yet even the stream into which you
step a second time
is not the one you stepped into before.
— Heraclitus

13

> Man is the only being
> who can overcome himself.
> His method is the Lie.
> What makes one man
> different from another
> are the glorious possibilities
> his lies contain.
>
> — *Hyatt*

We have reached a point where most of us would destroy the world in order to keep our *"POINT"* of view. Weak men must destroy, not for the joy of renewal, but for the catechisms of their tradition.

Humanistic and scientific definitions that saved man from blind faith and dependence have placed him in the hands of a "devil" more horrifying than the God he murdered. God is dead—but what has taken his place?

We are now seeing the children of transition. A new walking wounded, more vengeful, and hateful than lustful. A *new* race of Zombies—not the living dead, but the *dead living*. These creatures are the offspring of our dead God and his tradition. In this sense their presence is a hopeful sign. Something new is about to be born. But first we must live through an ugliness—a world of rotting corpses.

Unless our modern attitude is tempered by the irrational, man may become the servant of a new and even more horrible God—a binary scientific bureaucracy—whose primary purpose is the *illusion* of control and order. This new God can be likened to a piece of fruit that has a skin of proper shape but when squeezed, collapses—empty of juice.

The universal compulsion to gather and exchange "information" has led to a short-hand, a technical language, which has all but exterminated the object that it has attempted to describe. We now live more in image and form than in the complex realities we claim we "understand."

We have begun to mistake our fictions and labels for *life* and are taking these conveniences as *truths*, rather than living within our complexity and insecurity. If this process continues we will soon de-mystify ourselves—and create a de-humanization that will make the years of Hitler look like a rehearsal for a bad play. If God is *not* dead, man's refusal to live in his plenitude (insecurity) will drive Him to commit suicide.

DEAD YUPPIE →

A RACE OF ZOMBIES

*I challenge the reader to discern if anything Hyatt
has said, or for that matter anyone else has said, took
place while they were standing on their head.*

— *Hyatt*

THE ANTI-ZOMBIE THESIS

The foundation of all pathology is *nihilism* as a general
psychological state of experience.

Nihilism occurs when all ideological systems collapse—
and this includes the *cereal* meanings generated by culture.
The normal person avoids the extreme feelings of nihilism
by desperately clinging to those meanings and values implanted by culture, childhood and a weak biology, regardless of how irrational, painful and dull these meaning systems seem to be.

Healing occurs when the person regains his feelings of
power and reinstates his ability to create *meaning structures*. This theory is based on Friedrich Nietzsche's observation that the world is a work of art, created by the self.

The "pathological" person is a failed artist, while the
"normal" person has *accepted* consensual art and, in this
sense, does not own the concept of personhood. In this context it is important to constantly keep in mind that the *person himself is the work of art*.

Healing occurs in the will to create and form the world
and self as one's own creation. The feeling of power, and
the rational application of it to the ends of ones own creation, is the primary reflection of health.

WORKING THE ZOMBIE

The greatest danger of rationality and logic is not in the
method but in substituting the method for life. To apply
rational and logical processes to solve a problem is one
thing—but to try to live within a rational model is not living. Life, with all its hell and joys, *must* be an adventure in
order to remain human.

Life inherently is a-rational. It is whole and chaotic. It can only be "taken apart" for a peek. What we see is only a dislodged part—how we live is whole. The attempt to make life safe for breeding and for the meager indulgences of housewives has created this new race of Zombies.

Division is simply a convenience for fulfilling the desire to control—to have more for less. But it is this "less" that is the lie, the ultimate illusion. This "less" is a lie greater than any lie ever told. There is no way to have "more" for "less." Even God gave up his solitude for "more." The earth and the sky and the heaven are one. To divide them for convenience is one thing—to act as if this division were truth is another.

The facts are that with all this "more" we have "less." We have become so rational, so logical, so full of self-satisfaction that we are empty.

Yet, in this search for more individuality—more form—we find even less and less of life. People are as empty in their individuality as they are in their collectivity.

People feel an absence to the point that they must drown themselves in a world of addictions. An interesting quality about addiction, however, is that it offers the person a chance to have the experience of re-birth. It allows him to change—with justification. Recovery from an addiction allows a person to change and "gives" him permission to do things which would ordinarily disrupt his relations to those around him. (Keep in mind that most people do not want anyone to change.) He has hit bottom. He must learn to say *no*. Much like a transpersonal crisis, recovery makes a person special and unique. He has *overcome*. He has done something *special*.

Addictions are created in order to be cured. People need to feel and not to feel—desperately they want more in order to pay for their debts of the past. The addiction I am referring to is called—*form*.

The process of substituting form for essence can only continue for so long—ten years, twenty or one-hundred years. Sooner, rather than later, the machine collapses and, with the collapse, comes the potential for recovery.

We see the emptiness of dogma, the emptiness of ritual, the true Pharisee—the middle class—lost in form and circumstances, clutching desperately to symbols. We begin to realize that form cannot replace substance. We begin to realize that grand ideals, assertions and "acting-out" are not enough. We begin to realize that the Zombie is not just within but also without.

Still, we do not yet fully appreciate the depths of this depression—this emptiness—waiting not so silently behind us and in front of us. Yes, there is a new force on the horizon—a new cry for life. There is a strong desire to put an end to this non-living—this powerlessness—this non-purpose. The Zombie is waiting for a great thunder-storm—to be reborn.

However, neither crying nor waiting will help—

It is the time to be bold—to dance on the edge of the abyss—to fly again—where?

BECOME WHO YOU ARE

THERE ARE NO GUARANTEES

INTRODUCTION

By Robert Anton Wilson, Ph.D.

I remember the first time I entered Alternate Reality and accepted a lie as fact. I was five or six years old at the time and my parents had taken me to see a wonderful movie called *The Wizard of Oz*. Toward the end of the film there was a scene in which the Wicked Witch of the West, riding her broom, wrote in the sky like one of the mysterious sky-writing airplanes that I was accustomed to seeing. The airplanes always wrote the same strange message—*I.J. FOX FINE FURS*—but the Wicked Witch wrote something far different and absolutely terrifying. She wrote:

SURRENDER
DOROTHY

I was so frightened that I burst into tears. My parents had a hell of a job quieting me down, and I must have annoyed all the adults in the theater. Today, over 50 years later, I understand better what had happened. Sitting in the dark, staring at the movie screen, I had crossed the line between "reality" and "fantasy"—a line that is not nearly as firm for a child as it is (or seems to be) for an adult. Dorothy's danger, up there on the screen, was more "real" than my safety, down in the dark audience. This may or may not qualify as an imprinting experience in the Lorenzian sense, but it was traumatic in the Freudian sense. Even today, as I typed the terrible words "Surrender Dorothy," I felt a reflex shudder pass through me.

Well, a few years later I was able to distinguish movies from "real" reality. I watched the Frankenstein monster wreak havoc on the villagers, King Kong run amok in New York, Lon Chaney, Jr. turn into a werewolf, and none of it fooled me. I was amused at the younger kids who screamed during these films, or closed their eyes "in the scary parts." Still—only my conscious ego, or forebrain, was immune to the hypnosis. I still jumped when the director pulled his shock scene.

Watching adult audiences these days, none of whom believe literally in Indiana Jones or the Temple of Doom, or even in Batman and Joker, I see that, whatever they *think* they know, parts of their old brain, and of their bodies, still enter hypnosis easily. That's why they gasp, and cringe, and breathe hard, and have similar physical reactions, when things get rough up there on the silver screen. I can still see these reactions in myself, too, of course.

Only a small part of our brains, or our "selves," is able to resist the lies of a good artist. Nobody can sit through *Alien*, I would wager, without at least one sound of fear or distress escaping their lips during that "ordeal"...which consists only of looking at pictures projected on a screen...

A movie theater is the best place to learn the true meaning of Plato's parable of the prisoners in the cave, who accept shadows as reality. Every artist who moves us, from a movie maker to Beethoven or Shakespeare, is a bit of a hypnotist.

In this sense that seemingly stupid and mechanical contraption we call "society" must rank as the greatest artist on the planet. For instance, when I was seven or eight, and feeling superior to the kids who closed their eyes "during the scary parts," I was entering a deep hypnosis created by another Virtual Reality called language. This hypnosis was a worse nightmare than the Wicked Witch of the West or King Kong or the Wolf-Man or any of their kith and kin, but it made me a "member of society"—and "a member of the Body of Christ" as well.

The hypnosis was performed by the good and pious nuns at the school to which my parents sent me. Every day, school began with a prayer. After lunch, there was another prayer. When lessons were finished for the day, before they let us go, there was another prayer. Five days a week, September to June every year, for eight years, these prayers formed my consciousness into a Catholic mold. They were reinforced by Religious Knowledge class, in which we memorized the catechism, containing all the dogmas of the church. We had to pass examinations on that, just like we did in arithmetic, as if the two subjects were equally valid.

The result of all these prayers and all that memorization was that I came to dwell in a Virtual Reality in which a nasty old man living on a cloud a few miles above Earth was watching me all the time and would probably charbroil me or roast me or toast me if he ever caught me doing anything he didn't like. He was called God. He had a partner, even nastier, called Satan, who presided over the charbroiling and roasting and toasting, in caverns that honeycomb the hollow Earth. Between the two of them, God and Satan, life was far more terrifying than any "horror movie."

As a result of all the lies the nuns told me, I became a pretty good liar myself. When it came time for high school, I convinced my parents I wanted to be an engineer. That persuaded them to send me to Brooklyn Technical High School, and I didn't have to listen to the nuns drone on about God and Satan and Hell and all that horror movie stuff anymore. That was my real goal—getting out of the Catholic nexus. I didn't want to become an engineer at all.

At seventeen I became a Trotskyist. That was hot stuff in New York in the late 1940s. We Trots were more radical than anybody, or we thought we were. Of course, I was lying to myself again. Who the hell knows enough, at seventeen, to make an intelligent or informed choice among competing political ideologies? I had picked Trotskyism because one part of my mind was still Catholic and needed a hierarchy; the Central Committee made a good substitute for the Vatican. It allowed me to feel modern, scientific, "altruistic," brave, rebellious etc. and it did all my thinking for me.

At eighteen I quit The Party just before they could expel me. I pledged allegiance to the principles of individualism, free thought and agnosticism. From now on, I said, I will not by hypnotized by groups: I will think for myself. Naturally, I then spent over 20 years following various intellectual and political fads, always convinced I had at last escaped group conditioning and finally started "really" thinking for myself. I went from Agnosticism back to dogmatic atheism, and then to Buddhism; I bounced from Existentialism to New Left Activism to New Age Mysticism and back to Agnosticism. The carousel turned around and around but I never found a way to stop it and get off.

All this, mind you, occurred within the network of *language—the Virtual Reality created by the strange symbol-making capacity of the upper quarter inch of our front brain.* Language created God and Satan and Hell, in my childhood, and it created Liberty and Equality and Justice and Natural Law and other fictions that obsessed me at other stages of my "development." Language creates spooks that get into our heads and hypnotize us.

It is obvious, once one considers the subject at all, that our eyes cannot see the whole universe. They can't even see the whole room in which we happen to be sitting (they only see what is front of us, and not all of that...) Similarly, our stomachs cannot swallow the whole universe, and our brain cannot "know" the whole universe (they only know the signals they have received up to this second, and do not remember all of them consciously...)

Nonetheless, language programs us to try to speak, or to accidentally give the impression that we are trying to speak, as if we possessed the kind of infallibility claimed by the Pope or the Central Committee of a Marxist party. That is, language allows us to say things like "The rose is red," and in the mild hypnosis of this Virtual Reality we then promptly forget that the rose is more and other than red—

that it is fragrant, for example, and that it is temporary and will wither soon, and that it is made of electrons, which are made of quarks, and that it "is" only *red* to creatures with eyes like ours, etc.

Every over-simplification becomes a lie quickly (if we are not very cynical about language); ergo, language always lies, just because it over-simplifies. From "The rose is red" to "The National Debt forces us to raise taxes again" to "ARKANSAS MOM RAPED BY MIDGETS FROM MARS" to "Pornography is murder" (A. Dworkin) we proceed from one fiction to another, every time we open our mouths to speak.

(See my *Quantum Psychology*, New Falcon Publications, 1990, for further examples of how language creates a Virtual Reality experienced as just as real as a bottle of beer and a ham sandwich.)

Is it is possible to use language to undo the hallucinations created by language? The task seems impossible, but Zen riddles, Sufi jokes, the works of Aleister Crowley, and a few heroic efforts by philosophers such as Nietzsche and Wittgenstein seem able to jolt readers awake—shake them out of the hypnosis of words. The following book by Dr. Hyatt also makes that gallant effort to use words to transcend words. Success in this field does not depend on the author alone, however. It requires not only the right words, but the right reader at the right time, before the shock and awakening can occur.

Will it work for you? I don't know, but the odds of a favorable outcome increase if you do not "browse" or "skim" but read and re-read carefully, meditating all the while on the following two propositions:

1. Words can never say what words can never say.

2. With the right reader at the right time, words *can*, in fact, say what they can never say.

One of those propositions is the most dangerous lie in this book. Can you see which one it is?

LIE ZERO

The Tree of Lies

To Take Joy In Yourself
Is The Greatest Crime.

INSTRUCTIONS

When you read the Lies that follow, choose a number from 1 to 5 to indicate the strength of your reaction.

For example, the number 1 indicates that you had a weak reaction to a particular Lie.

The number 5 indicates that you had a strong reaction to a particular Lie.

The number 3 indicates neither a strong nor a weak reaction but somewhere in the middle. Please keep in mind that it makes no difference that your reaction is positive or negative. I am only concerned about the *strength* of your reactions.

After your first reading wait at least one week and go over the Lies and your reactions again. Rate them again. Note in particular any Lie which has a change of 2 points or more. This indicates that some fundamental "nerve" is undergoing transformation.

Rate the Lies when you are feeling strong. Rate them again when you are feeling weak. Feel free to make as many copies of them as you wish. Use your responses to build a journal around your moods and state of mind. Really get to know yourself.

Lies with ranks of (1) or (5) should be studied again and again. These reactions may indicate areas where personal work is required. Begin to ask yourself how you might *benefit* from your reactions. For example, if you rated the second Lie (5), how does your reaction benefit you? Does it help you avoid dealing with your desire to be seen or envied? Remember, most people react from an unconscious and emotionally based "moral philosophy" which they have not explored in detail.

When you repeat your own personal Lies, think about their origin or the purpose they serve. Conversely, each time you get to the roots of your Lies, no matter how uncomfortable, you become stronger and stronger.

An example might be useful to demonstrate the idea of "personal benefit." Bill gave Lie number three a rank of (5). When he was asked why, he said he "didn't like it." His second response was more to the point: he didn't like the feeling of insecurity he experienced, knowing that most promises assume a constancy that doesn't exist in the real world. This idea made him feel anxious, thus explaining why he had, in the past, built an entire morality on extracting promises from others and himself.

The majority of the Lies presented below come from my own "self-talk." The "parties" involved in these internal conversations have been influenced by many "outsiders." I have done my best not to steal any of these Lies and if in the future it is found that I am a thief let me now ask for forgiveness.

Each phrase I utter unlocks
the gates of heaven and hell

The purpose of every Koan
is to free you of all Koans

I am—others are—life is?
If you can answer these questions honestly you
have discovered the fountain of change.

THE LIES

1) My ultimate goal is to perish in the pursuit of myself.

1   2   3   4   5
Weak   Strong

2) Everyone desires to be seen, just so long as they are envied.

1   2   3   4   5
Weak   Strong

3) Every promise is a lie.

1   2   3   4   5
Weak   Strong

4) The spiritual health of a man is diagnosable to the degree he relies on morality as an explanation for his actions.

1   2   3   4   5
Weak   Strong

5) Religious freedom is an oxymoron.

1   2   3   4   5
Weak   Strong

6) You know you have found the right answer if it first offends you.

1   2   3   4   5
Weak   Strong

7) The anatomy of the sexes is simple: women are all soul and men are all heels.

1   2   3   4   5
Weak   Strong

8) The desire for constancy is the mother of morality. Who is its father?

1   2   3   4   5
Weak   Strong

RELIGIOUS
FREEDOM IS AN
OXYMORON

9) The father of the lie is childhood.

1	2	3	4	5
Weak				Strong

10) What teeth are to a tiger deception is to women and children. Deception is always the price of slavery.

1	2	3	4	5
Weak				Strong

11) Shame is admitting that we desire applause from people we despise.

1	2	3	4	5
Weak				Strong

12) The ultimate price for male superiority is femininity.

1	2	3	4	5
Weak				Strong

13) There is no easy way to become ordinary. You have to be born into it.

1	2	3	4	5
Weak				Strong

14) Just because men are similar doesn't mean that they are the same.

1	2	3	4	5
Weak				Strong

15) Teach nothing to anyone unless you're willing to suffer from it later.

1	2	3	4	5
Weak				Strong

16) Only a man who can choose from whom he receives applause is worth applauding.

1	2	3	4	5
Weak				Strong

17) What I pray for most is a fit God to worship.

1	2	3	4	5
Weak				Strong

18) The value of a shepherd is determined by his flock. Thus, no leader is worthy of envy.

1	2	3	4	5
Weak				Strong

19) There is nothing like a footnote to give a fool a place to stand.

1	2	3	4	5
Weak				Strong

20) Even a brilliant idea like the U.S. Constitution can be ruined by bad company.

1	2	3	4	5
Weak				Strong

21) We are all asked to participate in the same crimes. This we call law.

1	2	3	4	5
Weak				Strong

22) Morality allows the exploited the opportunity to feel noble.

1	2	3	4	5
Weak				Strong

23) The sins of the father are heaped on the son by way of the mother.

1	2	3	4	5
Weak				Strong

24) The best way to measure a man is to give him what he wants.

1	2	3	4	5
Weak				Strong

25) Punishment is a crutch which morality must endure.

1	2	3	4	5
Weak				Strong

26) Pain is a necessary condition of punishment, however, it is not sufficient. In addition to pain, what is necessary is the victim's consent that it is justified.

1	2	3	4	5
Weak				Strong

27) The most humane thing to do for a dying man is to convince him that he served a noble purpose.

1	2	3	4	5
Weak				Strong

28) Who can worship a God who knows His next Move?

1	2	3	4	5
Weak				Strong

29) Those desperate for applause can never hear it.

1	2	3	4	5
Weak				Strong

30) No other animal on this planet is so desperate for something to compare himself to that he invented god.

1	2	3	4	5
Weak				Strong

31) If you desire to be raved about never ask anyone to do it unless you pay them.

1	2	3	4	5
Weak				Strong

32) Self acceptance is based on self contempt.

1	2	3	4	5
Weak				Strong

33) There are no paradoxes in nature.

1	2	3	4	5
Weak				Strong

34) When I compare myself to another man I am either feeling superior or searching for justice.

1	2	3	4	5
Weak				Strong

35) What is the relationship between morality and orality?
The mouth.

1	2	3	4	5
Weak				Strong

36) The belief in truth began with a lie. What is that lie?
A) That truth is necessary and B) That a description is an
explanation.

1	2	3	4	5
Weak				Strong

37) You know nothing unless you can apply it.

1	2	3	4	5
Weak				Strong

38) To name someone is to claim them, thus the power of
parenthood.

1	2	3	4	5
Weak				Strong

39) What does a sheep know of wool?

1	2	3	4	5
Weak				Strong

40) Do not fear the serpent who needs to bite more than
once.

1	2	3	4	5
Weak				Strong

41) Morality soothes the pain of life by providing the victim with a sense of superiority.

1	2	3	4	5
Weak				Strong

42) There is a fine balance between people feeling grateful
or contemptuous when in the presence of someone they
regard as superior.

1	2	3	4	5
Weak				Strong

THE MAJORITY OF MEN HAVE BEEN
DEALT CARDS TO A GAME THEY
DO NOT KNOW HOW TO PLAY

43) When I am feeling strong I have no need to ask questions of myself.

1	2	3	4	5
Weak				Strong

44) The majority of men have been dealt cards to a game which they do not know how to play.

1	2	3	4	5
Weak				Strong

45) The question, "What future can we expect?" is a guarantee that the future is not possible.

1	2	3	4	5
Weak				Strong

46) I am angered that anyone from the Mid-West thinks they understand those of us who live on the edge.

1	2	3	4	5
Weak				Strong

47) Why are people so terrified of strangers? Most have forgotten that they were raised by two of them.

1	2	3	4	5
Weak				Strong

48) The best cure for misery is to learn to endure pain.

1	2	3	4	5
Weak				Strong

49) There is only one universal social law—obedience.

1	2	3	4	5
Weak				Strong

50) Knowledge is the original sin for the priest and the politician. Why? It sends them to the unemployment line.

1	2	3	4	5
Weak				Strong

51) The stupid and the brilliant believe they are the standard for everything: thus my fear of democracy.

1	2	3	4	5
Weak				Strong

52) Never trust a man shuffling without a full deck.

1	2	3	4	5
Weak				Strong

53) In order for an inequitable system to survive it must be believed to be ordained by God: which, of course, it is.

1	2	3	4	5
Weak				Strong

54) Lies are closer to the point than truth. They convey what someone is trying to hide.

1	2	3	4	5
Weak				Strong

55) Everything I despise is a statement of my esteem.

1	2	3	4	5
Weak				Strong

56) The fool, the priest and the bureaucrat are fascinated with averages.

1	2	3	4	5
Weak				Strong

57) There is no issue until you propose one.

1	2	3	4	5
Weak				Strong

58) Concepts are like helium balloons; they float higher and higher until they shrivel and fall.

1	2	3	4	5
Weak				Strong

59) One thing which makes man different from animals is he is forever comparing himself to his inventions and finds himself wanting.

1	2	3	4	5
Weak				Strong

60) Man is the missing link. We know who is on his left side but who is on his right?

1	2	3	4	5
Weak				Strong

61) Men flock together to protect themselves from wolves, never realizing that their greatest enemy is the shepherd and the flock.

1	2	3	4	5
Weak				Strong

62) Whether there are two choices or a hundred, the next one is always heresy.

1	2	3	4	5
Weak				Strong

63) It is up to each person to decide to whom he owes the truth.

1	2	3	4	5
Weak				Strong

ALL MORALITY RELIES ON THE SENSE OF SMELL

64) By pulling the leaves off a tree you won't expose its roots.

1	2	3	4	5
Weak				Strong

65) In order for an inequitable system to survive it must be believed that most people will turn their heads away. Thus all morality relies on the sense of smell.

1	2	3	4	5
Weak				Strong

66) Credit, Alcohol and Christianity—three legal drugs in America.

1	2	3	4	5
Weak				Strong

67) To believe that pain can be avoided not only causes misery, but makes you weak.

1	2	3	4	5
Weak				Strong

68) Everyone who claims that he is an altruist is guilty of counterfeiting.

1	2	3	4	5
Weak				Strong

69) A humanist is one who cannot tolerate being violated without advance notice.

1	2	3	4	5
Weak				Strong

70) To believe that love is more than proximity is to deny the reality of war and adultery.

1	2	3	4	5
Weak				Strong

71) It is amazing how biology transforms itself into philosophy.

1	2	3	4	5
Weak				Strong

72) To reproduce is the only imperative.

1	2	3	4	5
Weak				Strong

73) What most people want guaranteed is poison to a hardy soul.

1	2	3	4	5
Weak				Strong

74) Who can love a God who pities and loathes his finest creation?

1	2	3	4	5
Weak				Strong

75) Morality is sowed at the Breast and reaped on the Body.

1	2	3	4	5
Weak				Strong

76) Every plan assumes constancy: thus the belief in progress.

1	2	3	4	5
Weak				Strong

77) The only difference between hiring a thug or a lawyer to settle your affairs is of the senses; one is unsightly and the other smells.

1	2	3	4	5
Weak				Strong

78) When someone tells you that they trust you be on guard; you are soon to be violated.

1	2	3	4	5
Weak				Strong

79) Capitalism works for those with capital.

1	2	3	4	5
Weak				Strong

80) Freedom of the press belongs to those who own a press.

1	2	3	4	5
Weak				Strong

81) Justice belongs to those who make the scales.

1	2	3	4	5
Weak				Strong

82) To be in awe of Life is the only true religion.

1	2	3	4	5
Weak				Strong

83) Beware of the man who claims to be free. He is about to commit suicide.

1	2	3	4	5
Weak				Strong

84) The entire base on which Western Civilization and its religious humanism rests is the prevention of pain and the guarantee. The final payment for this insurance policy is slavery.

1	2	3	4	5
Weak				Strong

85) The value of a man's word or for that matter a government's currency are determined by how well they can tolerate uncertainty. Thus, weak currency and fascism sleep in the same bed.

1	2	3	4	5
Weak				Strong

86) The greatest danger to a budding genius is the middle class who are pulling him up by their boot straps.

1	2	3	4	5
Weak				Strong

87) A man who learns how to benefit from pain and adversity becomes stronger and stronger; thus, the need for pity and bureaucracy.

1   2   3   4   5
Weak   Strong

88) My greatest pain? When a woman rejects me for God. My next greatest pain? When a man rejects me because I am Godly.

1   2   3   4   5
Weak   Strong

89) To respect a man's opinion is to simply acknowledge that he had a mother.

1   2   3   4   5
Weak   Strong

90) It is now obvious that Hitler was unsuccessful in awakening us to the horrors of which normal men are capable. Thus, if we believe in progress, what might the next lesson be?

1   2   3   4   5
Weak   Strong

91) In order to understand Hitler you simply have to understand your neighbor, or for that matter, yourself.

1   2   3   4   5
Weak   Strong

92) Laws allow lawyers to send their sons to Harvard while yours go to City College.

1   2   3   4   5
Weak   Strong

93) Justice for the man in the street is simply someone to blame for his most recent discomfort.

1   2   3   4   5
Weak   Strong

94) If the weak and helpless didn't exist lawyers and politicians would invent them. How else could the middle class be exploited?

1	2	3	4	5
Weak				Strong

95) For most men the veil between opinion and hope is opaque.

1	2	3	4	5
Weak				Strong

96) The ultimate goal of Christianity and Socialism is: Earth as Asylum.

1	2	3	4	5
Weak				Strong

97) Like sleeping pills most opinions are designed to put the user to sleep.

1	2	3	4	5
Weak				Strong

98) The halls of divorce courts are paved with high hopes, romantic feelings and promises. What claims do any of these have on human decency?

1	2	3	4	5
Weak				Strong

99) Civilization is nothing more than a disguised form of genocide.

1	2	3	4	5
Weak				Strong

100) The criminal is indispensable to a society dominated by the politician.

1	2	3	4	5
Weak				Strong

101) Where Christianity goes, the Hangman follows. Science, however, has given us the atomic bomb and the electric chair.

1	2	3	4	5
Weak				Strong

CIVILIZATION IS NOTHING BUT A DISGUISED FORM OF GENOCIDE

102) Those who need to trust are either infants or cowards. If you cannot tolerate disappointment you cannot tolerate life.

1	2	3	4	5
Weak				Strong

103) Just because you find a fly in the ointment doesn't mean it won't soothe your wounds.

1	2	3	4	5
Weak				Strong

104) Once you give something a name you have made it public and all at once everybody thinks they know what you mean.

1	2	3	4	5
Weak				Strong

105) When someone is in pain over your decision—blame them.

1	2	3	4	5
Weak				Strong

106) When someone says, "it's your problem" it means that they can't bear their own.

1	2	3	4	5
Weak				Strong

107) Saying "I hear you," means "I need to say something."

1	2	3	4	5
Weak				Strong

108) Expect everything and nothing from everyone. This way you will not be disappointed: you will just be alive.

1	2	3	4	5
Weak				Strong

109) If you need to trust others you lack confidence in yourself.

1   2   3   4   5
Weak   Strong

110) There is nothing more dangerous than a person who believes he is independent.

1   2   3   4   5
Weak   Strong

111) Fine philosophies reflect more the need to feel good than how anyone has lived their lives.

1   2   3   4   5
Weak   Strong

112) Ethics and justice were created to expedite dealings between equally greedy and powerful people. If this is true, what is the common man doing with it? Taking revenge on his enemies!

1   2   3   4   5
Weak   Strong

113) I have been fooled the most by people who have helped me.

1   2   3   4   5
Weak   Strong

114) We cannot blame the survival instinct for human misery. We can blame human misery for the philosophies which condemn man's survival instinct.

1   2   3   4   5
Weak   Strong

115) Man cannot claim to be an animal: they couldn't stomach him. Man cannot claim to be a God: they have already excreted him.

1   2   3   4   5
Weak   Strong

116) Like a beggar, learn to ask; and like a beggar get up early.

1	2	3	4	5
Weak				Strong

117) Most questions are the intrusions of a coward.

1	2	3	4	5
Weak				Strong

118) What makes man different from other animals? No other species can create concepts which enslave them.

1	2	3	4	5
Weak				Strong

119) The need to verbalize, write and communicate are the basis of consciousness and slavery.

1	2	3	4	5
Weak				Strong

120) There are very few of us who do not turn our habits into virtues. There are even fewer of us who do not turn necessity into free will.

1	2	3	4	5
Weak				Strong

121) The system works if *you* benefit from it.

1	2	3	4	5
Weak				Strong

122) Self reliance is the enemy of all men in power.

1	2	3	4	5
Weak				Strong

123) We only create moralities, ethics and philosophies when we are out of touch with our instincts.

1	2	3	4	5
Weak				Strong

124) Man lives in constant terror of death. The proof of this is the time he spends appearing confident.

1	2	3	4	5
Weak				Strong

125) Never believe your own marketing plan.

1	2	3	4	5
Weak				Strong

126) I can guarantee nothing.

1	2	3	4	5
Weak				Strong

127) When people are strong they can enjoy each other. When they are weak they simply resent each other.

1	2	3	4	5
Weak				Strong

128) I am always amused by those who claim to love mankind; they are forever figuring out new ways to enslave him.

1	2	3	4	5
Weak				Strong

129) It takes a special kind of species to substitute pen and ink for blood and get better results.

1	2	3	4	5
Weak				Strong

130) I am defined by those I look up to and by those I look down on. Now you know why I live in shame.

1	2	3	4	5
Weak				Strong

131) If men were not guilty of crimes against women they wouldn't have difficulty in saying "no" to them without asserting their maleness.

1	2	3	4	5
Weak				Strong

132) Constancy and predictability are illusions required by other people.

1	2	3	4	5
Weak				Strong

133) I pity women who believe that in order to be free they have to imitate men.

1	2	3	4	5
Weak				Strong

134) The stronger the State the weaker the culture.

1	2	3	4	5
Weak				Strong

135) Death has no fear of man; it simply wants to avoid him for as long as possible.

1	2	3	4	5
Weak				Strong

136) Believing in good and evil is cynicism.

1	2	3	4	5
Weak				Strong

137) The brotherhood of man is death.

1	2	3	4	5
Weak				Strong

138) What would you call a man who creates Gods and then claims *they* deceived him? Ordinary.

1	2	3	4	5
Weak				Strong

139) What would you call a man who charges for his services and mistrusts you because you charge more for yours? Ordinary.

1	2	3	4	5
Weak				Strong

140) Ordinary men are the standard for all things. Extra-ordinary men shudder at the thought of being a standard for anything.

1	2	3	4	5
Weak				Strong

141) An inferior man is one who needs to know why you like him. He then decides whether he is deceiving you or you are deceiving him.

1	2	3	4	5
Weak				Strong

142) All arguments are simply disagreements on who needs more attention.

1	2	3	4	5
Weak				Strong

143) The worst pain I have seen is when an extraordinary man desires to be ordinary.

1	2	3	4	5
Weak				Strong

144) The more rules a person needs in order to live, the weaker the person. Might this also apply to Nations?

1	2	3	4	5
Weak				Strong

145) Man is at his best when he is actively striving not to be man.

1	2	3	4	5
Weak				Strong

146) Without morality deception and truth-telling are unnecessary.

1	2	3	4	5
Weak				Strong

147) The illusion that we understand each other is created by making the unique common. This is the mystery of language.

1	2	3	4	5
Weak				Strong

THE ECONOMICS OF SIN

148) What would it take for one Christian to pay off all his debts? The bankruptcy of the world.

1	2	3	4	5
Weak				Strong

149) Inflation is the result of getting others to pay for your sins.

1	2	3	4	5
Weak				Strong

150) Depression is the result of paying for someone else's sins.

1	2	3	4	5
Weak				Strong

151) Recession is nothing more than indecision.

1	2	3	4	5
Weak				Strong

152) It is often said by conservatives that in life, "you get nothing for nothing." Rarely does anyone tell you that it is often more true that you get "nothing for something."

1	2	3	4	5
Weak				Strong

153) Language has the uncanny ability of distilling the spirit out of life; yet everyone is drunk on it.

1	2	3	4	5
Weak				Strong

154) The word "I" refers more to a hope than a reality.

1	2	3	4	5
Weak				Strong

155) In America even authenticity is a means to an end.

1	2	3	4	5
Weak				Strong

156) The ego is the part of us which makes promises which the rest of the body can't pay for.

1	2	3	4	5
Weak				Strong

157) There are no hierarchies in nature: only relationships.

1	2	3	4	5
Weak				Strong

158) To take pride in serving as a well-dressed function is the ultimate goal of the middle class.

1	2	3	4	5
Weak				Strong

159) If you need to be forgiven you will steal again.

1	2	3	4	5
Weak				Strong

160) The ego is the self-reflective part of us which has the power to make alterations in someone else's plans.

1	2	3	4	5
Weak				Strong

161) If you wait around to be validated you will wait a long time.

1	2	3	4	5
Weak				Strong

162) The ego and the body are one. The first is born out of hope, the latter out of lust; one is a liar.

1	2	3	4	5
Weak				Strong

163) Everything becomes less important after I have obtained it.

1	2	3	4	5
Weak				Strong

IF YOU NEED TO BE FORGIVEN,
THEN YOU WILL STEAL AGAIN

164) Some men are forever turning others into resources and claiming that they are seeking friendship.

1	2	3	4	5
Weak				Strong

165) America died when it made heroism illegal.

1	2	3	4	5
Weak				Strong

166) A weak leader needs many rules. And a weak Nation needs many leaders.

1	2	3	4	5
Weak				Strong

167) Only a few people can truly give without feeling taken from. The reason? Their fullness pains them.

1	2	3	4	5
Weak				Strong

168) Never trust a god or a man who claims he has made a sacrifice. He is serving something he loathes and soon you will pay his debt.

1	2	3	4	5
Weak				Strong

169) To regret a decision is to believe that you already knew the future.

1	2	3	4	5
Weak				Strong

170) I have never met a man with tenure that I liked.

1	2	3	4	5
Weak				Strong

171) Next to the priest, the professional and his wife live off the pain they have created.

1	2	3	4	5
Weak				Strong

172) The greatest weakness is the demand to be considered by others.

1	2	3	4	5
Weak				Strong

173) Self-hate is the highest form of egotism.

1	2	3	4	5
Weak				Strong

174) If I showed you my enemies you would not respect me.

1	2	3	4	5
Weak				Strong

175) When you place someone before you, fear is your next step. Why? You have divided falsely. The solution? Learn multiplication.

1	2	3	4	5
Weak				Strong

176) To feel obligated to another is to negate their true will.

1	2	3	4	5
Weak				Strong

177) People like people who make them feel good; however, they rarely trust them.

1	2	3	4	5
Weak				Strong

178) Grateful people will surely pay you back.

1	2	3	4	5
Weak				Strong

179) Saving face bears no interest.

1	2	3	4	5
Weak				Strong

180) Never forgive someone for not knowing what they do; forgive them for believing that they do know what they do.

1	2	3	4	5
Weak				Strong

181) The inferior man's method of extracting consideration is always at someone else's expense.

1	2	3	4	5
Weak				Strong

182) Forgiveness is like a handshake. You have to do it
every time you meet.

1	2	3	4	5
Weak				Strong

183) Man is so self-centered that he spends more than half
of his life resenting others and the other half resenting himself.

1	2	3	4	5
Weak				Strong

184) A man who needs to be trusted doubts himself more
than anyone else.

1	2	3	4	5
Weak				Strong

185) Simply because you can predict or control an event
doesn't mean you understand it.

1	2	3	4	5
Weak				Strong

186) I have neither plans nor goals, but simply frustrations.

1	2	3	4	5
Weak				Strong

187) To believe in opposites is to ignore differences.

1	2	3	4	5
Weak				Strong

188) Hedonism and Puritanism sleep in the same bed.
Why? Both wish to be free of the pains of life; one in this
world and the other in the next. Thus, both are life negative.

1	2	3	4	5
Weak				Strong

189) Labels are a hypnotic; they delude you into believing that whatever was scaring you is now under your control.

1	2	3	4	5
Weak				Strong

190) The tools of a politician and a car salesman are the same: fear, greed and the "guarantee."

1	2	3	4	5
Weak				Strong

191) It will be horrifying to find out that our greatest philosophies are the result of a constipation.

1	2	3	4	5
Weak				Strong

192) If you wish to understand how history is made observe how you live.

1	2	3	4	5
Weak				Strong

193) What scares me most about humans is the belief that they *are*.

1	2	3	4	5
Weak				Strong

194) It is amazing how far we have come while knowing so little. It is even more amazing how little we have changed while believing that we know so much.

1	2	3	4	5
Weak				Strong

195) It has been said that man first believed in the powers of magic. When that failed he tried religion. When that failed he tried science. What's next?

1	2	3	4	5
Weak				Strong

196) Man's attraction to ritual magic and science is the belief that he can discover the truth and manipulate it according to his will. One of these is a lie.

1	2	3	4	5
Weak				Strong

197) Religion opposes both magic and science. Religion holds that only God knows the truth and that man must plead with God to spare him from it.

1	2	3	4	5
Weak				Strong

198) My greatest "altruistic" acts have been the result of instinct.

1	2	3	4	5
Weak				Strong

199) Equality is the vision of a man frustrated by the breast of his mother.

1	2	3	4	5
Weak				Strong

200) Peace is for the dead, strife is for the foolish and tranquillity is for the wise. Is this the fifth lie?

1	2	3	4	5
Weak				Strong

201) I only trust myself when I am silent.

1	2	3	4	5
Weak				Strong

202) A man willing to argue at the drop of a hat is a man in need of constant reassurance.

1	2	3	4	5
Weak				Strong

203) Those who have the power to define have all power.

1	2	3	4	5
Weak				Strong

204) Does a true skeptic leave a place for truth?

1	2	3	4	5
Weak				Strong

205) Every judgment is simply the result of a value system held in place by violence.

1	2	3	4	5
Weak				Strong

206) How can you claim that men are equal in the eyes of God and claim that God exists?

1	2	3	4	5
Weak				Strong

207) Reason is the whore of desire.

1	2	3	4	5
Weak				Strong

208) If a man could have every desire gratified instantaneously he would be a horror to behold.

1	2	3	4	5
Weak				Strong

209) What makes the law legal? Guns.

1	2	3	4	5
Weak				Strong

210) Man has the uncanny ability to make accident and necessity into a choice.

1	2	3	4	5
Weak				Strong

211) You will die—unless science says differently.

1	2	3	4	5
Weak				Strong

212) Every blessing becomes a curse, but rarely does a curse have the potential of becoming a blessing.

1	2	3	4	5
Weak				Strong

213) The trouble with asking a man to rely on his experience is similar to asking a caterpillar to fly: you have to rely on metamorphosis.

1	2	3	4	5
Weak				Strong

214) Is it a coincidence that life improves with the loss of memory?

1	2	3	4	5
Weak				Strong

215) Who requires the belief that they are in control? Someone who is not in charge.

1	2	3	4	5
Weak				Strong

216) Justice and causality are the drugs of choice for insomnia.

1	2	3	4	5
Weak				Strong

217) The American economy should thank God for Newton's law of inertia.

1	2	3	4	5
Weak				Strong

218) It takes little more than silence to make most men tremble.

1	2	3	4	5
Weak				Strong

219) In a democracy each opposing vote cancels each other out. Thus it is possible for one vote to decide an election. Is there any significance to this?

1	2	3	4	5
Weak				Strong

220) Self-importance can be defined as building a giant fortress believing that its size is keeping others away rather than their lack of interest.

1   2   3   4   5
Weak   Strong

221) No one can hide anything; every lie, every deception is reflected in the body.

1   2   3   4   5
Weak   Strong

222) As I get weaker I have less and less to prove and more and more to show for it.

1   2   3   4   5
Weak   Strong

223) Only those who have failed to live need to have virtues.

1   2   3   4   5
Weak   Strong

224) The type of solution proposed by government to remedy a problem exposes the depravity and ignorance of its citizenry. Thus, we can *war* against flies and pills.

1   2   3   4   5
Weak   Strong

225) The only way you can take daily life seriously is to suffer from a bad memory.

1   2   3   4   5
Weak   Strong

226) Greedy men have a difficult time in overcoming a first impression.

1   2   3   4   5
Weak   Strong

227) I would much prefer to be murdered with passion than killed by a briefcase.

1	2	3	4	5
Weak				Strong

228) Only Gods and men are foolish enough to make promises.

1	2	3	4	5
Weak				Strong

229) I have been asked over and over again who are the weak of the world. They are not the ones starving or the ones living in the street. They are the ones who are fearful of starving or living in the street.

1	2	3	4	5
Weak				Strong

230) The middle class are those who think they have a lot to protect and believe they have the right to rely on someone else to protect it for them.

1	2	3	4	5
Weak				Strong

231) Every living thing on the planet is compelled to reproduce itself. Man is the only creature who believes that it is a conscious choice.

1	2	3	4	5
Weak				Strong

232) Less then 1% of the world's population are creators. The balance are simply consumers who believe that they have the right to the creator's genius.

1	2	3	4	5
Weak				Strong

233) A lawyer is a moral bulimic.

1	2	3	4	5
Weak				Strong

234) Class is the ability to treat your servants with an air of kindness and respect.

1	2	3	4	5
Weak				Strong

A LAWYER IS A
MORAL BULIMIC

235) The types of criminals a society creates betrays the depth of its virtue.

1	2	3	4	5
Weak				Strong

236) I am overwhelmed by people who have no sense of history. I am even more overwhelmed by people who have no sense of accident.

1	2	3	4	5
Weak				Strong

237) A man with nothing left to lose has everything to gain.

1	2	3	4	5
Weak				Strong

238) Only men require women to be unfathomable.

1	2	3	4	5
Weak				Strong

239) Once this book is published it will be on its own—you will only know it by its smell.

1	2	3	4	5
Weak				Strong

240) What is dirty about the word power? Its conditionality, its dependence on others assent to it by their weakness. Power can only be beautiful when it is unconditional—dependent on no one.

1	2	3	4	5
Weak				Strong

241) Heroism is for the survivors.

1	2	3	4	5
Weak				Strong

242) Every man is immortal until his mother dies.

1	2	3	4	5
Weak				Strong

243) Mourning is only for living.

1	2	3	4	5
Weak				Strong

244) Our body is incapable of doing what our mind desires.

1	2	3	4	5
Weak				Strong

245) While the body dies only the ego is preoccupied with death.

1	2	3	4	5
Weak				Strong

246) One of the distinguishing characteristics of pride is death.

1	2	3	4	5
Weak				Strong

247) There are no secrets. If you know yourself, you know what everybody else is "hiding."

1	2	3	4	5
Weak				Strong

248) The truth is simple—everything IS as perfect as it can be for a species such as this.

1	2	3	4	5
Weak				Strong

249) When you lack purpose you will either become an optimist or pessimist.

1	2	3	4	5
Weak				Strong

250) When death is conquered only then will we be more than animals.

1	2	3	4	5
Weak				Strong

Only those
who live from the belly
CAN TAKE ADVANTAGE OF BOTH ENDS

Some individuals have read these Lies and laughed, others have read them and cried: some have liked a few while others have liked a lot of them. But most individuals have *not* followed the instructions to rank each one. Did you?

If you follow the instructions and come back to your responses in a few days you will begin to see how your reactions have changed. This procedure will provide an opportunity to know yourself better. Your reactions will tell you where you stand and why you stand there.

BECOME WHO YOU ARE

THERE ARE NO GUARANTEES

THE FIRST LESSON IN LYING

The Way To Learn To Lie Is To Assert

AND SO, WE START WITH...A SYSTEM

There is no better way to learn than by doing, so come into the process of making the lie. First, we assert...

NERVEENA
THE FOUR SUPREME TRUTHS

1• All is Joy
2• The Origin of Joy Is Division
3• Joy is the Result of Union
4• The Infinite Fold Path Leads to Joy

1• All is Joy
2• The Origin of Joy Is Division
3• Joy is the Result of Union
4• The Infinite Fold Path Leads to Joy

1• All is Joy
2• The Origin of Joy Is Division
3• Joy is the Result of Union
4• The Infinite Fold Path Leads to Joy

1• All is Joy
2• The Origin of Joy Is Division
3• Joy is the Result of Union
4• The Infinite Fold Path Leads to Joy

If you are not yet convinced, simply assert this louder and louder. Or, better yet, just go to your computer and push "PASTE."

And now, into the "system..."

THE SUPREME PATH

1. All particles come together in love yet remain separate.
2. The Formula of Love is Tension (Yod[1]), Charge (Heh), Discharge (Vau), and Relaxation (Heh).
3. All things are unequal thus everything is in harmony.
4. Turn every obstacle into your advantage.
5. Suffer only in action.
6. Action is the only Sacrament.
7. Do not Lament over Division.
8. Have Great Desires.
9. Take Great Risks.
10. Learn Silence.
11. Worship the Chameleon.
12. Be Willful and Deliberate
13. Pity is Disrespect.
14. Nothing is Good Enough for Me.
15. Everyone is the Center of the World.

Joy and Love are enemies of IHVH. The study of the most divine formula of *TCDR* proves the point:

All that man can know is known through his *Nerves*. Hence, memorize the following and apply it everyday: (T)-tension-(C)-charge-(D)-discharge-(R)-relaxation = 233: Ayin, Tsaddi, Cheth, Heh, Yod, Yod, Mem = Tree of Life. Now 233 reduces to the number 8 meaning in Hebrew *To Will* and the Hebrew word for *Pleasures of Love*. Or more

---

[1] Yod, Heh, Vau and Heh (IHVH) are the Hebrew letters which represent the secret name of God in the system of mysticisim known as Qaballah. From this comes the word *Jehovah*. Every Hebrew letter is also associated with a numeric value. Through the mechanism of *Gematria*, words which "add up" to the same numeric value are associated with each other.

simply Love Under Will. Now, at this point we must be very careful. There is a series of words which have 8 letters which gives the whole "gag" away. They are—*it is as if.* These 8 letters can change the whole world. If you practice this formula everyday for a year you will become one of the first humans on this planet.

The application of this formula leads to: *Nerveena*—however *Nerveena* is Active *and* Passive.

The tropistic formula *is* the message. There is no death—only orgasm. Choose well—between a beautiful woman or God. To make images—to imagine—is Sin. Our motto: Sin often.

There is no intrinsic wisdom in language.

Nothing is hidden in language, unless of course you have substituted language for your heart and guts.

Life cannot be expressed by the subject-verb-predicate—myth. The key to myth is that by its use you can make slaves. We have been taught to respond to the language (the media) rather than the message. (John did not go to the store. Sally did not see Spot run. Jack did not fall down the hill.) Unfortunately, the media has become the message. If we wish to survive with dignity the message must remain the message. Kill the media.

The actor, the act and the object are only *devices*. The brain does not experience the actor—the act—the object. It experiences the whole scene. (This includes filling in what led up to the scene and what will happen afterwards.) Then a part of the brain uses language to communicate the scene to itself and others. The communication of the scene is responded to as if it *were* the experience of the scene. The method of communication is not the scene: Kill the Zombie. Do not let the Zombie—stand in the way of your brain.

Communication is always *tense.*

Communication is always—the other, self as other.

Communication is always—the black mirror.

With lan(gauge) we establish logic and consistency. This does not mean that consistency and logic exist in the scene in the way lan(gauge) has presented it. "All likes are alike —is true." But no-thing is like any-thing. Note: here the word true can only be referring to consistency.

If you have understood what I have just written you have missed the point.

System building is fun—whether it is true or not is of *no importance*.

System building (organized lying) applies to all groups which spring up around dead men. Once the leader is gone his spirit does not remain for long. Sooner or later the group becomes simply form. For example, look at the groups which have followed in the footsteps of Nietzsche and Crowley. They are shallow and academic, worshipping petty rules and regulations. They lack power and inspiration. Like a coffin they contain only the withering remains.

BECOME WHO YOU ARE

THERE ARE NO GUARANTEES

LIE ONE AND ONE/HALF

The Worst Lies Of All Are About You—
Your Mind Belongs To The Priests

> *If you wish to be loved*
> *Dare not put your will before Gods,*
> *The States, Your Parents or, for that matter, Anyone.*
> *— Hyatt, talking to a person who feels unloved, 1977*

The worst lies ever told have been about you. Anytime anyone said anything about you they lied. No one can truly know anything about you—including yourself. Others only know what appears on their "computer screen." You only know what appears on your "computer screen."

The most critical lies were told about you when you had minimal critical faculties—when you were young. These are the scripts others wrote for you. We call these scripts "traditions." While it is difficult to know otherwise, you are not *inherently* your experiences or conclusions.

> *Like Frankenstein's creature, you have been made.*
> *Thus, we are all the monster.*

More powerful lies were "performed on you" before you even knew about lies. These are non-verbal lies.

No one knows what humans are and no one knows what humans should be—without God there is no standard. This is your chance—to be Zombie or not.

Non-verbal lies are the building blocks that allowed other people to build models of you. They are lies that live in the body and are later reinforced by words. These models are the basis of all self-fulfilling prophecies. *We have all been molded of clay.*

All humans interpret events in terms of metaphysical models. *An unpleasant experience is compounded by an unpleasant conclusion. A pleasant experience is compounded by a pleasant conclusion.* All conclusions (generalities) based on specific experiences are lies. When repeated long enough they appear true.

We are all handicapped by our traditions and conclusions.

The notion of a metaphysical self that is either good or evil—defined by other people's subjective needs and desires—tell us more about other people's needs then our own-self.

These conclusions about self are without independent existence, yet they deeply affect how we interpret the world and ourselves.

Since bad and good things will still happen regardless of what we do, we find ourselves arranging these experiences into pre-existing models that have been implanted in our head. Our salvation, however, is at hand. We can save ourselves by saying, "I don't know."

At a minimum there are two levels of experience which are confused by almost everyone: *direct experience*—like a brick falling on your head—and the *interpretive conclusion* of the event. The first experience is wholistic, the second is a combination of past models, attribution needs, and anxiety. The feeling components of these two experiences can become indistinguishable. Therefore, a model is difficult to remove because it has become associated with the feeling component. As feeling cannot be completely denied, the models which interpret the *meaning* of the feeling also cannot be denied. Not only are these models difficult to change, the model often becomes independent of further experience and "causes" the feeling. This further "proves" to the person the validity of the model.

Although thoughts do not "cause" feelings they do elicit them. "Positive thinking" cannot be effective unless the underlying metaphysical "feeling" models are in accordance with the positive thoughts. Models run on automatic.

Models can't be made to coincide with positive thoughts because of the simple fact that "bad" things happen no matter *what* thoughts a person has. The solution to this is simple—accept bad experiences without having to have an explanation or a conclusion. If the unpleasant feelings do not disappear within a short period of time, you know that the experience is being upheld by a model which has metaphysical implications about your self-worth and your competency in the world.

While all too human, our attempt to prevent "bad" experiences is futile. It is this desire which has led to the worst dictatorships in history. It has also led to what we now call "civilization"—which is nothing more than organized cowardice and laziness.

Model building is an exciting activity, however, the models we build as children are too personal. We generalize these models to the universe at large, disregarding context and time. This causes no end of grief. We hold on to these models even when we know cognitively that they are flawed. The very fact that we are alive is somehow seen as proof that these models are valid.

As a species we have not easily learned to think contextually or probabilistically—instead we think in discrete categories. Generalities about self and life give us an illusion of security regardless of the error and misery they cause us. For example, we have a difficult time coping with disappointment when we don't have a satisfactory model to explain it. When we have a model—any model—we feel better, even though the model may be in error and we still don't have what we want. Most people would rather "understand" than live.

Every individual is superior to any disembodied concept used to describe him. I say *superior*, not superior *and* inferior, since I give the individual priority over any and *all* concepts.

No rule is greater than the context which violates it.

Like justice, the metaphysics of personhood is nonsense—serving, like justice, an illusion to quiet the souls of those who have to label themselves and others metaphysically to reduce anxiety and feel at peace.

Metaphysical damnation, as well as metaphysical affirmation, are the common drugs of the masses—they are a poor substitute for a strong stomach and a good right hand.

Children are the primary victims of these lies. Not only are they told lies time and time again, they make them up. Almost everything people believe as grownups consists of lies they were told as children. Culture is *nothing more* than agreed upon lies.

Every conclusion is a lie. (If you sense a contradiction in this statement, note that my conclusion about conclusions is at a different level of abstraction—a meta-level.) Logic asserts that like cases are alike. This is fine, but in reality there are no "like cases." We only assume like cases for convenience. Logic applies to closed systems that allow us, by a process of elimination, to come up with the one right answer. In open systems logic fails—and rightfully so.

Nothing is ever over with and nothing is ever put to rest—things linger. A strong feeling or emotion about one event can bring a whole array of other thoughts and feelings into awareness. A failure in the present can bring forth an array of failures of the past. Every event feeds one or the other metaphysical notion—damnation or affirmation. However, things are not so simple. Some people only have damnation or non-damnation possibilities. Nothing ever affirms them. Others have only affirmation or non-affirmation possibilities,. Nothing ever damns them. The latter group is frequently regarded as "normal," while the former group is frequently regarded as "pathological." This division is false, since both groups (and the mixed group) are simply Zombies of a different flavor.

Other individuals flip/flop between high affirmation and high damnation. One moment they are everything, the next they are nothing. This is frequently associated with parents who used all-or-nothing metaphysical statements in a confused, alternating fashion when responding to specific behaviors.

BECOME WHO YOU ARE

THERE ARE NO GUARANTEES

LIE TWO

Joy Is Your Duty?
Your Body Belongs To The Priests

Are *men* living at all?

Blake shows us how he has described the world with language; we find such words as hate and love, reason and energy, heaven and hell.

His word-smithing goes unsurpassed, yet does he understand that language is simply lan(gauge)?—the thickness of the tongue? How can we gauge Blake's understanding? By how he lived his life?

THE LIFE FORCE

Without Contraries there is no progression. Attraction and Repulsion, Reason and Energy, Love and Hate, are necessary to Human existence.

From these contraries spring what the religious call
Good and Evil. Good is the passive that obeys Reason.
Evil is the active springing from Energy...
All Bibles or sacred codes have been the causes of the following Errors:
1. That Man has two real existing principles: Viz.: a Body and a Soul.
2. That Energy, call'd Evil, is alone from the Body; and that Reason, call'd Good, is alone from the Soul.
3. That God will torment Man in Eternity for following his Energies.
But the following Contraries to these are True:
1. Man has no Body distinct from his Soul ...
2. Energy is the only life, and is from the Body; and Reason is the bound...of Energy
3. Energy is Eternal Delight.
Those who restrain desire, do so because theirs is weak

enough to be restrained...
He who desires but acts not, breeds pestilence...
Joys impregnate, Sorrows bring forth...
Joys laugh not! Sorrows weep not!
Exuberance is beauty...
These two classes of men are always upon earth, and they
should be enemies: whoever tries to reconcile them seeks to
destroy existence. Religion is an endeavor to reconcile the
two. Note: Jesus Christ did not wish to unite, but to separate
them...and he says: 'I came not to send Peace, but a Sword.'
Opposition is True Friendship...
One Law for the Lion and Ox is Oppression.
             — *William Blake, The Marriage of Heaven and Hell*

Goethe finds no difficulty in telling us simply what must
be done. His ability to convey what he has observed has yet
to be surpassed. But to have lived with him would have
been better: that is, if you could have tolerated his habits.

All force strives forward to work far and wide
To live and grow and ever to expand;
Yet we are checked and thwarted on each side
By the world's flux and swept along like sand:
In this internal storm and outward tide
We hear a promise, hard to understand:
From the compulsion that all creature binds,
Who overcomes himself, his freedom finds.
             — *Goethe, The Mysteries*

Nietzsche provides us with a glimpse of the meaning of a
self-artist; someone who has made himself. Often he would
use Goethe, Socrates or Napoleon as examples of "giving
style" to oneself.

Self-style is self-discipline and not obedience.

The reader should underline the phrase "law of their
own" in the following piece.

One thing is needful. 'Giving style' to one's character—a
great and rare art! It is exercised by those who see all the
strengths and weaknesses of their own natures and then com-
prehend them in an artistic plan until everything appears as art
and reason, and even weakness delights the eye. Here a large
mass of second nature has been added; there a piece of original
nature has been removed: both by long practice and daily

labor. Here the ugly that could not be removed is hidden; there it has been reinterpreted and made sublime... It will be the strong and domineering natures who enjoy their finest gaiety in such compulsion, in such constraint and perfection under a law of their own; the passion of their tremendous will relents when confronted with stylized, conquered and serving nature; even when they have to build palaces and lay out gardens, they demur at giving nature a free hand.

Conversely, it is the weak characters without power over themselves who hate the constraint of style...they hate to serve. Such spirits...are always out to interpret themselves and their environment as free...nature—wild...arbitrary...fantastic, disorderly,...only in this way do they please themselves. For one thing is needful: that a human being attain his satisfaction with himself...only then is a human being at all tolerable to behold. Whoever is dissatisfied with himself is always ready to revenge himself therefore; we others will be his victims...

— Nietzsche, The Gay Science

DO YOU REALLY WANT THIS BODY?

We "live" in ...the most expedient form of terror.

"You respond to contemporary events without awareness that your past rather than the present is the basis of your reactions. Most people are 'set' to respond to present situations based on their level of psycho-physiologic arousal."

— Hyatt, reacting physiologically to a college professor.

The level of arousal is a function of internal states and external stimulation. Thus, all contemporary situations are void of independence. The entire world is set to respond from the traumas of the past. What is experienced as real is simply one's own level of arousal-tension and what is experienced as relief is *whatever* relieved the tension in the past. What people 'choose' are those acts which don't push a familiar state of arousal beyond its normal pattern for too long. Thus we can destroy the mystery of masochism along with paradox and leave them and reason in the dust. I pray with this truth that the Moolahs of the middle class—the hypocrite—shall perish from this earth.

— From Hyatt's dream where he was killed.

My nightmare freed me from thinking I could understand anyone without knowing their level of arousal and tolerance.

I was freed from the binds of love and hate—greed and need—acceptance or rejection. It freed me from my frequent observation that good things can and do cause bad things. Success can be a killer. I felt like a limp rubber band. I left my apartment feeling good—as the Zombie turns.

BECOME WHO YOU ARE

THERE ARE NO GUARANTEES

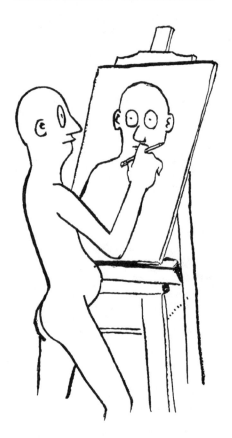

LIE TWO AND ONE/HALF

Responding To Metaphors

Our society is an animal with the head of a camel and the rear of a lion. John acts like a bull in a china shop. People act exactly like animals when they drink.

These are all metaphors which attempt to describe what a person sees and what a person feels under certain conditions. The statements themselves are non-scientific.

When we speak in metaphor we convey feeling, reaction and image. When someone challenges us rationally we sometimes will slip into explanations to cover our asses.

When we use such words as "society," "culture," and "mind" we believe we are speaking factually and not talking in metaphor. Society, culture and mind do not exist at the same level of concreteness as a swift kick in the ass. They are ideas that are associated with certain weak definitions and "personal" feelings.

When we speak of society we speak of a set of assertions which are publicly shared. Like waving a flag, spouting assertions gets people moving. A society is really a group of clichés based on selected fictions. In simple language a society is a construction. It does not have the same quality of "existence" as the individuals which make it up. Yet we respond to words with more intensity and feeling than we do to the sight of blood.

To understand what we call a society we simply have to look at its fictions. But before we study fictions in detail the first fiction we are told is that a particular set of fictions are not fictions.

As Americans our fictions are truths. Have you ever wondered why victims are sometimes blamed even more than the perpetrators? Well, the victim is the residue— proof of the imperfection of society's fictions. Fictions are solutions which don't work except as fictions. Most any set of fictions will do as long as it is accepted as *non-fiction*. Victims are fiction—failure. Thus, victims must be paid back for exposing the failure of the fiction.

Fictions tell us what to do, what to think, how to behave and what to feel. So far so good. However, things are not as simple as that. Fictions are often complex and contradictory. "All men are equal." "Everyone is an individual." These are contradictory at face value. The way they become non-contradictory is by creating a new fiction. "Everyone has equal rights in the eyes of the law." Once we invent a new fiction we can keep the fiction that "Everyone is an individual." Once this is done we can all go back to sleep— or can we?

Anyone with a mind (or experience) knows that everyone doesn't have "equal rights under the law." Everyone knows that due process is simply metaphysical jargon which refers to the act of processing—of form. (That is, in due time you will get yours.) It means nothing more.

How about the fiction of punishment? Does anyone hear from the government unless they are about to be punished? Very rarely. How many pretty blue and pink cars do you see with beautiful men and women handing out free lottery tickets for driving safely?

How many letters and phone calls do you get telling you that you did a good job? You only know about the government in bad times—your bad times. Why is it that you only need negative input? How come it is believed that you should rely on yourself and family for positive input? How come some people believe that people don't need input at all (except to be told that they are doing wrong—semi-Zombie.) Why doesn't the government give you a free lottery ticket for paying your taxes early? Why, because there is no lottery. But we all know that positive reinforcement is dangerous—we will take advantage—we the people will... This example illustrates that fiction is really believed. Citizens will not obey unless threatened. That is the truth. Citizens and governments have dissimilar interests. You only require punishment when you have to make someone do something against their best interests.

Positive feedback is the exception and not the rule. Even big business pays lip service to positive—authentic—feedback. Why is it that "no news means good news?" Is it simply a popular cliché?

As fictions become greater in number and more and more of the fictions become known as fictions people become anxious and restless. When fictions begin to collapse new fictions are required to reduce the anxiety caused by the loss of older fictions. For example, today we have Satanists and drugs undermining our youth. The problem is never the original lie, but someone or something undermining the "perfect order." We never discuss the error of our fictions.

A society is nothing more than a prescription for the human condition known as *existential presence*. The prescription is nowhere to be filled. There is no pharmacist. All we have are fictions to keep us safe. We have our humble beliefs and fantasies, our four walls and the sound of traffic.

We strive day to day for the fulfillment of our hopes, each day evaluating our success—often by the fact that we survived. But the fictions go on! Quietly we work, age and die. In between we have our few pleasures, a feeling of strength from time to time. Most often we have the simple things to soothe the desperation of our soul.

Our skin gets older, our belly fatter, our frame shorter, but we have our fictions to keep us warm. Every once in a while, we have fiction wars, battles paid for in blood to "prove" whose fictions are blessed by God. But we do not have to wait for war—death is all around us everywhere. One thing a society does know for sure is to remove "the dead" as quickly as possible. Appearance is everything for fiction addicts.

Today, in our modern world, we have introduced the fiction of addiction. Everything is addictive, including society. (One fiction upon another fiction.) What is *not* addictive? Living a normal life. What is that? Never substitute one need for another, always over-centralize, cope in constructive ways.............. These fictions seem to get heavier and heavier. Every lie requires more lies. And society is the greatest lie.

A normal life is satisfied with fictions and anonymity. It means saying one thing and doing another. It means that you are satisfied with very little. So normal people have a house, a partner who never dies, (then they become a widow(ER)), children who are never a problem, a job they go to everyday even though they hate it, a partner they sleep with even though they bore them. However, with all this "chosen" normality, more and more researchers are finding more and more people who are addicts or victims or perpetrators—or?

As we go deeper and deeper into normality we find adulteries, drug fiends, alcoholics, bulimics, gamblers, criminals, sex fiends, child abusers, child sex abusers, pornography, nicotine and coffee addiction: sweet addictions, TV, music, relationship, family addictions, sports, animal addicts, human rights addicts, work addicts, food addicts, computer addicts, prescription drug addicts, religion addicts, sleepwalking addicts, shoppers, credit card junkies, etc. Most everyone is an addict and everything is an addiction. Most everyone is a victim, a perpetrator, or all of the above. If you do not have an addiction you are pathological. If you are not a victim you are left out. If you are not a perpetrator you must not be male. Well, let's be serious. What I am saying is that we are all being discovered—but the system and the Moolah still hold on to their fictions—

their history books—and of course the book of bad deeds—
the bible. It is comforting to have something in your hand. I
much prefer my…

BECOME WHO YOU ARE

THERE ARE NO GUARANTEES

LIE THREE

The Earth As A Nursing Home

*In the late 1700's Goethe predicted that the planet
Earth would become a nursing home.*

But *before* Goethe's quote Nietzsche says,

> One has one's tiny pleasure for the day and one's tiny pleasure
> for the night—but one has a regard for health. One herd: each
> wants the same, each is the same—and whoever feels different
> goes voluntarily into an asylum.

Today's advertisements concerning mental health and
addiction confirm Nietzsche's prophecy.

The goal of the planet is to become a Nursing Home.

Is this the "Will of Nature?"

Why is it that most Utopias (including Hitler's Utopia)
appeal to the weak and the lame? And why are there so
many who wish for nothing more but relief? Is this what it
takes to buy votes—a promise to do away with life?

To kill the body and replace it with a computer chip?

The way I wrote the first paragraph gives the impression
that Nietzsche lived before Goethe. As a writer I must give
the reader the impression that I am accurate. One error
could destroy my credibility and make empty my hope to
achieve immortality through my writings.

Error allows the man secure in facts to criticize the man
who is able to tolerate more rejection. Remember what Vaihinger said in 1911, "...the most expedient form of error."
What Vaihinger meant by error was, of course, a distinction
between "truth" and what makes it easier for "us" to survive: fictions. The Moolah calls every comfort a truth.

I confess—I have deceived my reader—I couldn't find Goethe's quote. I simply remembered the feeling it created in me.

Having given up on finding Goethe's exact quote I began asking myself what are some of the qualities of a good nursing home. What came to mind is this:

In a good nursing home everybody is pampered all the time; everyone is competent immediately; everyone else is to blame for any unhappiness or frustration; and every-thing is easy and without blood.

I believe this is a good description of the ideal nursing home as well as much of the philosophy of the New Age. To sum up, the inhabitants of the Nursing Home—an abor-tion of Egotism and Weakness—a new child has arrived in Bethlehem. This child has No-Body.

At last I found the quote by accident—in two places.

This accident took seven months to the day—after read-ing 313 pages. I eagerly re-read Goethe's passage and compared it with my "memory." I was anxious to find out if someone would have discovered my error and punish me by publicly humiliating me.

Now for Goethe:

> Also, I must say myself, I think it true that humanity will triumph eventually, only I fear that at the same time the world will become a large hospital and each will become the other's humane nurse.
> *— from Goethe's letter to Frau von Stein, June 8, 1787.*

The reader will immediately detect how my memory dis-torted Goethe's quote to fit my peculiar spirit. But before being judged too harshly remember what Nietzsche said about truth, "all truths are for me soaked in blood." Does this mean that Nietzsche was blood thirsty? Or was he saying that all truth had to be suffered—lived—loved—made love with? Kill the Zombie and watch me bleed.

BECOME WHO YOU ARE
THERE ARE NO GUARANTEES

LIE FOUR

ARISTOTLE AS GREEK

ARISTOTLE AS ANTI-CHRIST

"A person is thought to be great-souled if he claims much and deserves much... He that claims less than he deserves is small-souled... The truly great-souled man must be a good man... Greatness of soul seems...a crowning ornament of all the virtues... Great honours accorded by persons of worth will afford [the great-souled man] pleasure in a moderate degree: he will feel he is receiving only what belongs to him, or even less, for no honour can be adequate to the merits of perfect virtue, yet all the same he will deign to accept their honours, because they have no greater tribute to offer him. Honour rendered by common people and on trivial grounds he will utterly despise, for this is not what he merits... He therefore to whom even honour is a small thing will be indifferent to other things as well. Hence great-souled men are thought to be haughty... The great-souled man is justified in despising other people—his estimates are correct; but most proud men have no good ground for their pride... He is fond of conferring benefits, but ashamed to receive them, because the former is a mark of superiority and the latter of inferiority. He returns a ser-

vice done to him with interest, since this will put the original benefactor into his debt in turn, and make him the party
benefited. The great-souled are said to have a good memory
for any benefit they have conferred, but a bad memory for
those which they have received (since the recipient of a
benefit is the inferior of his benefactor, whereas they desire
to be superior)... It is also characteristic of the great-souled
men never to ask help from others, or only with reluctance,
but to render aid willingly; and to be haughty towards men
of position and fortune, but courteous towards those of
moderate station...and to adopt a high manner with the
former is not ill-bred, but it is vulgar to lord it over humble
people... He must be open both in love and in hate, since
concealment shows timidity; and care more for the truth
than for what people will think; ...he is outspoken and
frank, except when speaking with ironical self-depreciation,
as he does to common people. He will be incapable of living at the will of another, unless a friend, since to do so is
slavish... He does not bear a grudge, for it is not a mark of
greatness of soul to recall things against people, especially
the wrongs they have done you, but rather to overlook
them. He is...not given to speaking evil himself, even of
his enemies, except when he deliberately intends to give
offence... Such then being the great-souled man, the corresponding character on the side of deficiency is the small-
souled man, and on that of excess the vain man."

And what might a vain man be? "Someone who deserves
little and demands a lot."

*Most everyone who has read Aristotle's brief on Great
Men feels uneasy. Why?*

The Greatest Revenge Is Success.

BECOME WHO YOU ARE

THERE ARE NO GUARANTEES

LIE FIVE

The Model Is The Message

The Model Is The Message—the image is devoid of fact.

The model(s)—paradigms—men use to tolerate their existential presence tells you more about them than the content of their message.

Trust more in a man's moods than in his thoughts.

Assertion: The better a man feels the less complex his models. The worse he feels the more complex his models. The real question—do complex models explain more of reality than simple ones? Or is complexity a poor model for describing the issue of models? Or am I misusing the concept?

What we need to look at is elegance.

The weaker a person the more binary his models. What do I really mean by this? As a rule weaker people think primarily in discrete one dimensional binary terms. They are stuck in a fascistic state of mind. This must be expected since their defenses are primitive.

Look at what has been done to the *whole brain model*. Weak minded people say that there *is* a left brain and a right brain. This type of "mind" does not even recognize that they are talking about a model. A stronger person says, *a model* of the brain is ....

A stronger and more knowledgeable person says, "a model of the brain based on Herrmann's work consists of 4 factors and not 2. The whole brain model has 4 primary components. They are left cortex, right cortex, left limbic system, and right limbic system." Which person is stronger? Which person is in a better mood? Do my assertions concerning moods, weakness and model complexity apply? If they do apply how do they apply? Or is my model simply based on poor observations and definitions?

Which model of the brain will sell more books and to whom? This might help us understand my model better. I will predict that the two brain model will sell more books and the people who buy and believe it will be more right brain and less left brain. A person high in mathematical ability and analytical reasoning would find the book a joke. A whole brain person might be interested in the book, buy it, but not believe it.

What sells is the model—not the product. The facts are that most of us live in a one dimensional, model discrete (yes/no) universe.

Some people can even tolerate *maybe*. How many people can tolerate a multi-factor interacting model? Very few. It would require that they specify conditions of when, who, where, and how. This is too much for most people. Their tolerance for existential presence is low.

Politicians and advertisers rely on the fact that most people only respond from a yes/no matrix. As people become more complex they add maybe. As they become more complex they add more and more factors. *Sooner or later they become organic and they look simple again. Complexity becomes a simple art form.*

BECOME WHO YOU ARE

THERE ARE NO GUARANTEES

LIE SIX

Feudalism Everywhere

If I have only one message to offer the world it is— Feudalism is alive and well—everywhere. The Neo-Lord knows that it is not necessary to own the person. It is cheaper to control everything the slave has and does and call it safety. As the body becomes more and more an "object" the feudal lords will simply pull more and more pieces from it.

Safety and security are the watchwords of the white-middle class—the wonder bread people, the Zombie people and their kids. Cowardice has become a virtue and elevated to a "moral necessity."

DEMOCRACY IS THE BEST FORM OF FEUDALISM (OWNERSHIP) EVER INVENTED.

IN THE END THERE WILL BE NO SACRED OR PROFANE—ONLY THE HARMLESS AND THE USEFUL.

BECOME WHO YOU ARE

THERE ARE NO GUARANTEES

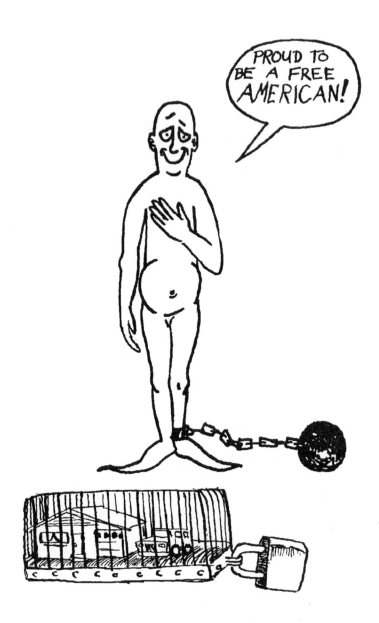

LIE SEVEN

Rebellion As Instinct

Way back in 1952 Dr. Robert Lindner was one of the first modern psychologist to suggest that *rebellion was an instinct* and *as necessary as the sex instinct for the survival of the species.*
Lindner believed that rebellion was normal and not a pathology.
Compare this idea to the one held concerning adolescent rebellion not to mention the rebellion of adults who refuse to live the dead-end cowardly existence of the wonder bread class.
Lindner was one of the first to directly warn that psychology would become a whore of the State and business. He felt that in time both the public and the psychology profession would begin to believe that psychotherapy had more to offer than it did. He also felt that psychology had become part of the "plague" of adjustment. His prediction has come true—unequivocally. Look at psychology today—with its ads for addictions, depression and co-dependency.
The purpose of psychology as practiced today is to make the person in trouble "passive." And this definition is fully in accord with Neo-Feudalism.
But Lindner's most important contribution was his statement that, for humanity to realize its true potential, it had to overcome the "triad of limitations": *gravity, ignorance* and *mortality.*
Lindner wrote this circa 1952, long before the pioneer Dr. Timothy Leary published his Space Migration, Increased Intelligence and Life Extension "goals" sometime in 1977

in *Exo-Psychology* (now revised and published as *Info-Psychology*, New Falcon Publications.)

Lindner also proposed a new morality, "Anything—thought or deed—which enables man to pierce the three-sided cage described by the *triad of limitations* is intrinsically good; anything which prevents him from so doing is intrinsically bad." He felt that this "new morality" was completely incompatible with the morality of the Moolah and the wonder bread people.

I had borrowed Lindner's book from my dear friend and mentor Dr. Israel Regardie, the rascal Guru, who said he had forgotten that he had it in his library and confessed that he had only "looked" at this book.

In 1991, while looking over Dr. Regardie's papers, I found correspondence between Lindner and Regardie. Apparently, Regardie "forgot?" that he and Lindner had exchanged a number of letters. In fact Regardie was quite taken with Lindner's ideas. Lindner complained that his book had been ignored. (In reading the Lindner-Regardie letters in detail we found that they exchanged information on a topic which bothered Dr. Regardie until the day he died. It appears that Regardie did not forget Lindner at all, but simply didn't want to discuss the relationship since it brought up some unpleasant feelings.)

Most great works go "unnoticed" particularly if they threaten the hypocrisy of the upper-middle and middle class parasite. For those who do not understand these parasites let me say that they are the ones who claim to be serving higher principles when in fact they are simply serving themselves. In essence they are cowards who seek power and status through conceptual deception.

Rebellion has always been a prime issue for me, but I had never conceptualized it in just the way Lindner did. His phrasing ("rebellion as instinct") seemed to hit me right where I lived. But the question remains—what was I rebelling against? Was it discipline? Or was it the demand that I give up my body's knowledge of itself and the world for someone's slogan?

I close this section with another quote from Lindner:

> "...the various psychotherapies have as their job the recovery of individuals and groups for evolution so that those whose lives would otherwise be wasted can also contribute toward the same end: the coming glorious breakthrough into...What?"

?

BECOME WHO YOU ARE

THERE ARE NO GUARANTEES

LIE EIGHT

There Is No Reality, Only Media Events

The solution to fiction is always more fiction: thus god invented man to listen to his stories.

I have been sworn "to tell the truth" We Owe Authority Everything

I was told to tell the truth even when it meant punishment.

I tried and failed.

As time went on I was told that to tell the truth in the hope of a reward meant that I was without moral fiber. I was told that I should tell the truth for "truths sake." I concluded that Truth was a jealous and horrible God. Then I read about Jesus who felt forsaken by God at the time of his greatest need. At that moment I knew that belief was even more horrible than truth.

I abandoned truth and belief—and fell in Love. As my arms drew Her to my chest I awoke from my dream holding my pillow. All at once I realized that truth, belief, and love were only sounds resonating in my pathetic brain. They had no reality but brain-reality.

I learned that auditory symbols "cause" autonomic reactions (emotions) and were the fundamental basis of human behavior.

Emotions convey a sense of solidness—a three-dimensionality to the brain—like a brick wall. I concluded that emotions could be made into "brain" walls simply by manipulating the sounds and symbols people respond to.

The only truth left was that I was always lying. This awe/ful fact—a "bad" memory, poor hearing, bad eyes and an aging sex drive—has made me very unreliable. I became a man of the moment, a man afflicted with moods. People mistook me for a Zen Master—until I yelled at them!

My inherent lack of reliability is only balanced by an equal resolve to suffer eternally from every promise that a moment of joy or terror has caused me to make.

You see, we all suffer from our desire to extend ourselves in time by making promises—a horrible substitute for immortality. Thus, I decided that I was either a saint, an artist or a philosopher. Regardless, I hold out no desire to be saved at the moment of my cruci-*fiction*. Thus, I have learned to "choose" my fictions wisely.

He Who Screams First!!!
NO-ONE IS INNOCENT

To assert is to prove. When someone says you wronged them—it is your duty to react and defend yourself.

This is an example of how form is substituted for fact. Why is there so much interest and anxiety when someone makes an accusation? Our minds have been trained to tacitly accept an accusation as a truth. We react this way because of the structural relationship of parent and child. The parent asserts—the child defends. Every assertion promotes fear. Thus, the idea of "innocent until proven guilty" is only a principle—it is not organic. We are all guilty even after we are proven innocent.

Humans are so weak that they require someone else to be guilty of the same things that they have done.

Regardless of how bright or intelligent, regardless of how developed, the one claiming victimage elicits a response from the crowd. We have all wronged and been wronged. We wait for someone to punish. When we hear an accusation our eyes light up. "It is him and not me."

We are all guilty of not being Christ-like. We are all guilty of not living up to the images of our childhood. We all claim superiority when we find a victim to suffer for us. We feel safe when someone else is being punished. Our sins go unnoticed for awhile.

Who would want to accuse? Someone who is wronged. Someone who didn't get what they "think" they deserved. I once saw a woman who later accused me of not being kind or understanding. "What an accusation!" I said to myself. So what. But the accusation became public. Eyes clicked from left to right. Everyone sat up in attention.

Many came to her defense. Many had been waiting to have reason to torture someone else. When my accusers told me what I was guilty of, they smiled. They waited for my reaction. This is what they wanted most of all—my reaction. What they received was a smile. I turned away—presenting them with my ass. This did not suit them. They confronted me again. I smiled again and walked away. After three times—they stopped accusing. After a month or two, however, they accused me again. This time I again smiled and turned away.

We are taught to meet every accusation with a defense. And we are taught that the best defense is a strong offense. Thus, we live in a world of accusation and counter-accusation. Whoever accuses best wins. Yet, many of us feel that the guilty party has gotten away. They have. Each of us is guilty of knowing that every accusation is a negotiation strategy. Every accusation is a lie.

The whole truth can't be seen lest we forgive everyone. Hatred and anger keeps empathy in check. If we feel empathy then we become weak. How to feel empathy and still kill? Be honest with yourself first. Know that everything is a violation of some principle. Learn to humanize your violations of others.

In our culture we live off each other while pretending to care for each other. Both activities are lies. We neither live well nor care well. For most of us life is simply form. We feel sorry for ourselves privately. Yet, publicly we claim innocence. We are all guilty of the crimes of childhood. And what is this crime? Being a child.

But, we are really guilty of something worse—remaining a child—not in our innocence—but in our laziness. We are too lazy to be human. It is easier to react like a beast. We are too lazy to go deep enough into anything. Being human means going deep—it means going beyond form—.

BECOME WHO YOU ARE

THERE ARE NO GUARANTEES

LIE NINE

Learning How To Faint

To understand an abstraction
Simply look at who uses it and how.
There is no mind without its body.

Freedom for the weak is simply freedom from...
Freedom for the middle class is both freedom from and freedom to... but only in moderation, of course.
Freedom for the great is unnecessary.

WHEN THOUGHT IS PURE IT IS DEAD
For the weak slavery becomes a virtue,
For the middle class slavery becomes a vice,
For the great slavery is simply a given.

If you wish to understand any concept ask yourself how it affects you. For example how do you feel when you use the concept Divine Providence, Justice, Love, etc.

Does the concept of "justice" make you feel strong when you have been harmed?

Does believing in a forgiving God make you feel warm and cozy when you have broken your marital vows?

Does believing in a revengeful God make you feel good when you are seeking revenge?

To understand an abstraction, ask who would prefer a God who forgives, and who would prefer a God who takes revenge?

What kind of spirit prefers which abstractions?

Who would like to sit next to God in an afterlife and watch their enemies punished?
Who needs to be granted liberty?
Who needs rights?
For that matter, who needs concepts?
Next ask, when do you use a particular concept?
When you feel strong?
When you feel weak?
When you feel helpless?
When you have harmed someone?
When someone has harmed you?
When you have the flu and wish you were dead?
When giving birth?
When dying?

WHEN THERE IS A PROBLEM
LOOK AT LANGUAGE AND NOT AT "REALITY"

The ability to reflect, to lie, to make metaphor, to paint pictures is as *natural* as the sex instinct. But, who for that matter defines natural and unnatural? What is the history of the use of the terms "natural" and "unnatural?" Who has used these terms and for what purposes? Who suffers from the mind/body problem? A man with neither?

WHEN A BAD MEMORY CAN'T FAIL

To label one quality of man natural and the other unnatural is proof of a very innovative labeler—to torture oneself over these labels is proof of a bad memory—.

We are the inventors of the ideas that create the problems that we feel helpless to solve. Who feels power and comfort in believing that we are living in "paradox?" Someone who makes money by solving riddles. These people are called politicians, philosophers, psychologists and priests.

As Korzybski has put it—natural and unnatural might better be described as assisted and unassisted nature. Many of man's sorrows are the result of being hoodwinked by his own melodies.

BECOME WHO YOU ARE

THERE ARE NO GUARANTEES

LIE TEN

Hope Is The Currency Of The Weak—
I Am Not An Optimist Or A Pessimist

Christianity and Communism.

I have despised both philosophies for so long that I have concluded that I am a closet advocate.

I require guarantees and forgiveness. Finding these abhorrent qualities in myself led me to the conclusion that my instinct for life was weak—I had the Zombie virus.

I believed that by fighting this disease in others I could ignore my own illness.

When I realized my folly I refused to be made a Zombie by the workings of my mind. I learned to let go of losing situations—quickly. I learned to lose. I learned to win.

My cure consisted in learning that suffering was inevitable—and *then saying "so-what?"*

Every priest, politician, psychologist and philosopher remains employed—in power—because people have been trained to believe that there is something wrong if they suffer.

There is nothing wrong with suffering—it is an existential condition.

We do not need Buddhism or Jungian Psychology or Positive Thinking or Leaders. We need our own organisity. We need to become an Art-Form.

After a short period of time my internal condition improved.

I overcame inertia.

I did this by turning every misfortune to an advantage.

My lies were getting better—more useful and powerful.

THE BEST LIES I'VE HEARD
THE PHILOSOPHIES OF OPTIMISM AND
PESSIMISM

Why would anyone need to be either an optimist or a pessimist?

Well, those who require an "attitude" in order to function.

They simply can't handle a body punch.

Living from a body of strength is not something most men can do.

They require a way to "look" at things.

What a man says has nothing to do with what he feels.

For example most people who state they are optimists are really pessimists. I have met people who claim to be pessimistic who fundamentally react from a place of hope. They simply have difficulty in dealing with disappointments. Many people believe that their attitude affects things and situations which can't be affected by attitude, such as a check arriving in the mail. They confuse attitude with "cause and effect."

People who need to discuss positive attitudes are normally depressives who are trying to get out of their depression. People who need to emphasize their pessimism or cynical attitude are usually very hopeful people who have felt devastated by disappointment. Some people have put me in that category—someone who has never overcome being disappointed.

When I gave up being an optimist and a pessimist I could not tolerate the anxiety.

So I labeled myself a realist.

Then an occultist.

Then an agnostic.

Finally, a Zombie.

As long as I had a label I was comfortable—for a while. When my view changed I experienced tension again. Soon

I became depressed—another word for being tense and tired.

I began watching the clock. I noticed that having a positive attitude was more important during the late afternoon and late evening. During the early morning and late morning I didn't need any labels. Conclusion: the stronger you feel the fewer labels you need.

BECOME WHO YOU ARE

THERE ARE NO GUARANTEES

LIE ELEVEN

A Decision For A Bureaucrat
Is Loss Of Job Security
For A King,
It Is An Adventure

Everyone with a Ph.D. is a binary fascist. (Note: begin to pay attention to your reactions to my assertions.)

The illusion of "inevitable conflict" has been transformed into a well paying profession for priests, politicians, philosophers and more recently for those who call themselves psychologists. I am a writer and do not get paid well!

The ability to create and perceive conflict and then provide solutions has led to occupations that provide security and respect. It is unfortunate that women are finding more and more opportunities in these once primarily male professions. Women would "fare" better in the future if they looked toward the arts and sciences.

Conflict only exists in a binary Universe.
Live in the immediate

Its not so much that pain hurts
What is worse is the meaning you give it

BECOME WHO YOU ARE

THERE ARE NO GUARANTEES

LIE TWELVE

Civilization Is Like A Condom: It Gives You The Impression That You Have Made Love

Civilization (pays for) utility and docility. Utility is the ability an individual "has" to function "as" a service. Docility is simply the payment an individual makes for being *allowed* to serve as a function.

EVERY WEAK MAN MUST BELIEVE IN THE MORAL NECESSITY OF HIS CATEGORIES. THIS IS BASED ON HIS INABILITY TO RELY ON HIS STRENGTH TO ENFORCE HIS OWN DESIRES ON HIMSELF.

I must warn the reader that I regard self-mastery and discipline to be as fundamental as the sex drive itself.

I do not regard self-mastery and discipline as alien or imposed from without but rather as *requirements* for art.

I, however, do differentiate the *absolute innate desire for self-mastery* from the horrors that civilization calls obedience.

Every exploiter assures us of his necessity. I for one am totally unnecessary.

What lets me know that I am unessential? When I remember that my body looks like an ape's. Rejoice in your unessential nature—if you can tolerate the freedom you feel.

BECOME WHO YOU ARE

THERE ARE NO GUARANTEES

LIE THIRTEEN

The Hero Today—
An Oxymoron For Tomorrow?

I pray over and over again to perish in the pursuit of a worthy goal. The moment I stop praying and act I have made Love with God.

In today's modern world the idea of the hero has become an oxymoron.

Everyone is an individual, everyone is important and the cry of everyone is the same: "YOU—give me more—now. Make it easy for me."

I have lied again.

What I have just said is not true—the farmer in the Mid-West still holds to the ideas of God, Country and Family in the face of the inevitable.

For the farmer, the hero is a man with no face (his face) who has upheld the values of the farmer.

The man in the city has his heroes too:—young police officers in pursuit of criminals—fair maidens—Wall Street Billionaires with slick greased hair and over-sized condoms.

YOU KNOW A MASTER BY HIS DISCIPLES
THIS IS WHY I LIVE IN SHAME

In the face of all these heroes how can my statement that "heroism in the modern world is an oxymoron" be true? You will know this answer when you can answer the question—*whose hero are you?*

117

Don't become too horrified when you find out.

YOU ALWAYS KNOW A MAN
BY THE CHARITIES HE KEEPS
I GIVE MY MONEY TO BIO-CHEMISTRY

Certainly, there is someone who looks up to you?

Who admires you? It may be a child, a mate, a parent, a teacher, a friend, or for that matter everyone you know. No doubt you are a hero for someone—think about it for a moment or two—*who* are you a hero for?

The next question is why are you thought of as a hero? There are as many answers as there are people. Please list three *virtues* before you go on:

1.

2.

3.

Knowing for whom you are a hero—can be a source of great shame.

BECOME WHO YOU ARE

THERE ARE NO GUARANTEES

LIE FOURTEEN

What If Hitler Was Accepted Into College?

*The reason why most people do not change is because they do not **hate** themselves enough.*

There is no way of knowing how a disappointment will affect history.

The study of Hitler reveals one simple fact: once you study Hitler there is no longer any need to study politics.

The Hitler episode is the one and only "course" necessary to understand the very complex subject called "political science." Another phrase for political science: overcompensation for an inferiority complex.

Most members of the human species are herd animals. Similar to domesticated sheep and cows they contentedly and proudly strut to the market to be slaughtered.

Unlike other herd animals, however, humans believe they are individuals with a free-will and a mind of their own.

Humans can't tolerate insecurity, disappointment, or frustration very well.

Like many others, Hitler knew this fact very well. What was Hitler's regime—The—*We Mentality*.

Security Programs—Identification with a Hero—Guarantees—Someone To Blame for Misfortune—Freedom as Obedience—Enemies—A Sense of Superiority Based on the "We"—Sacrifice for the "We."

What embarrassed mankind so much about Hitler's existence? He showed them how capable they were. He showed them what an inferior person could do when sufficiently angered.

He showed the Moolah what he would do to protect his house. Hitler turned the idea of a rational, humanistic mankind into a joke. He showed us how the most normal and decent man could be made to run a gas chamber.

TERRORS OF THE HERD
EVERY HERD ANIMAL
HAS GIVEN UP HIS BODY FOR A FENCE

What terrifies an animal who has been declawed and defanged? An animal with claws, fangs and a can opener.

Herds want to feel safe.

What makes the herd valuable? Utility and docility. Once the herd loses utility or docility they are of little value.

No one is loved "for themselves" in a herd.

The herd has been told that it is honored for its servility and loyalty. It is told that it is superior because they spout the philosophy of pity and kindness. Yet, their kindness is simply a necessity—for what else can a frightened animal be? What terrifies the herd animal? Everything.

What is the herd animal's argument against living? Everything.

BECOME WHO YOU ARE

THERE ARE NO GUARANTEES

LIE FIFTEEN

Jesus As Hero

For whose Sins did he die?
A strong man requires no one to die for him.

"By your deeds ye shall be known."
Jesus a hero?
He died for the sins of the world sayest the slaves.
I say, "who in the hell asked him?"
I have it on good report that he was executed for his own sins, his rebellion against the prevailing authorities. This too is a lie.
Who would require someone else to die for them?
Jesus the hero?
Is this an Oxymoron?
Jesus?
Where does his heroism come from?
Dying!
Well we all do that.
To die voluntarily?
Well, my physician died when he dove into the raging Pacific Ocean trying to save his two drowning daughters.
When I heard of his gesture, I felt that I had known a God.
But I missed him. Maybe he didn't know that his gesture was doomed to failure. Maybe he thought he could beat the howling waves of the Hawaiian coast. Maybe he couldn't live with himself if he didn't try. I don't know what I would have done.

Probably something different. I once saved a little girl from drowning, but that was in a swimming pool.

According to Hebrew tradition I didn't get a good mark for this since my life wasn't in jeopardy. Maybe Jesus was a Jew who read the same book on Hebrew tradition that I did. So, maybe Jesus' dying for the sins of the world got him a good mark in his Father's Book?

But who in hell asked him?

Heroes are often thought to be military types or individuals having extraordinary skills or abilities.

What skills did Jesus have?

He was a carpenter.

He was a hypnotist.

What values did he uphold by his death?

The ability to resist the senses?

The ability to hate the body?

Oh! He was a Jewish physician who didn't charge.

Who worships the man without a penis?

Old women, children and animals?

How many people deliberately die and claim they did it for someone else?

And why does dying for your own values become a virtue?

Why would a human being want to worship someone like Jesus?

What kind of human being would do this?

If you sacrifice your life for a value you uphold how can your death be sacrifice?

If you sacrifice your life for something you loathe then...........?

I know I am grateful that Jesus died for me. Does that mean that I don't have to die?

As the king of endarkment, Jesus became an ideal wonder story for Paul etc. to build another empire for the slaves.

A hero is someone who does something extraordinary (makes a sacrifice or risks) for someone else, whether this someone else is a person, a group, a God, or a country.

But who would remember a man who sacrificed his life to save a dog from being run over by a car? The dog's owner, maybe?

Jesus died for 18% of mankind.

So, Jesus is a failure. He didn't get 50% of the vote.

The more extraordinary and the greater the number of people who know of you, and/or are thought to benefit from your act, the greater the hero you will be.

In fact people require heroes whether their heroes play football or murder people in different colored clothing (military heroism).

Intellectual or scientific heroes are less important to the masses. For example, compare Salk with the average football star. Or compare Einstein to Jesus. Einstein is often a model Jewish parents use to make their sons feel guilty and inadequate. How many mothers use Jesus in the same way?

As you can see, popularity is an important factor in heroism, so one must always ask the question—hero to whom? Thus, heroism may be simply a function of the "physics of mass." It may also be, as in the case of Jesus, a compensation for boredom and organ inferiority.

Another purpose of the hero is to convey immortality (indestructibility) for the people who admire him.

Thus, can we say that Jesus was an immortalist?

Or was Jesus just a bad copy of Dionysus?

The force and power of the hero is always transferred to the people who create him.

Does this explain Jesus' heroism? People's need for someone to love and be loved by?

Who needs unconditional love? A baby or an old person. Or a victim.

Give me a warm body—not a corpse.

Was Jesus the first Zombie?

If I offered immortality to Jesus would he take me up on it? No. Like many of us Jesus needed to prove something to himself. I wonder if he did?

BECOME WHO YOU ARE

THERE ARE NO GUARANTEES

LIE SIXTEEN

Surrender Or Else

(From *Sex Magick, Tantra & Tarot: The Way of the Secret Lover,* 1996, New Falcon Publications.)

Intuitively we all know that to love and be loved is both the spark and fuel of life. But how does a mortal surrender to love when fear is so pervasive in our lives? Without love life feels empty and meaningless. It is unfortunate but true that most of life's miseries are caused by our inability to surrender to love. In a desperate attempt to fill this void people become addicted to alcohol, food, sex, endless affairs, fame, fortune and, of course, drugs.

Frequently the use of love substitutes is not simply an attempt to deaden pain but is also an attempt to bridge the gap of separateness and join with the Beloved. In Western Civilization the preoccupation with these "substitutes" is "proof" that our society doesn't really concern itself with love and surrender. In fact much of Western psychology regards the desire to unite with the Beloved as pathological. In the West love is dangerous until it is licensed like a car.

SURRENDER IS NAUGHT

One of the primary obstacles to surrendering is the mistaken belief that you can actually "lose" yourself. This fear is based on a deep primal feeling that to love and be loved is a form of "cannibalism."

The desire to consume the love object and thereby merge with the beloved has been a romantic image that poets and lovers throughout ages have struggled with.

Though the boundaries of the individual must necessarily fade away, there is no way in the world that you can lose your Self. Your true Self is *hard-wired in* and even if it were possible to lose one's self or be possessed it would have to be the result of one's true will.

One real danger in love relationships is that most people secretly believe that they must control the love object in order to feel safe in loving and being loved. The cause of this is simple—children are made to feel that they must "give themselves up" if they are to be loved. Thus, for most humans the act of surrender has meant the loss of autonomy. Or worse—loss of one's own mind.

Surrender is neither control or morbid dependency and can't be made contingent upon giving away your "soul"; although the person surrendering opens himself completely to the moment, and does run the risk of being deeply hurt.

Sadly, in our society this is not uncommon and frequently serves to harden or embitter a person toward life in general. Or, on the other hand being deeply hurt in the act of surrender can lead to angry and painful "cries for help." When this occurs there is an insatiable and wrathful desire to be cared for as a child is cared for *and* the horrid fear of loss of independence.

Similar to the innate will for self mastery, the *will to surrender* has been exploited by religion, government and even the family. Far too frequently when little children surrender to their parents they are humiliated, shamed or even worse. When they become adults they, in turn, do the same to their children.

Radio and television are constantly attempting to exploit the desperate need for love. In their perverse forms of "entertainment" they create hysteria, foster the anti-life morality of collectivism and sell "pornography" as love.

They peddle their perverted ideas of romantic love and sexual union as ecstasy but their fiat currency cannot fill the hearts and loins of their viewers. The world still yearns for a love which few of us know. And this love is beyond anything any one individual can satisfy, yet at the same time this love can only be actualized through the love of another living person.

Much of psychopathology and many physical ailments are the result of the inability of the individual to surrender, to let go completely…to merge momentarily; be it with a person, divinity or one's own "secret lover." This is one purpose of this book, to help you discover your *will to surrender.*

Most so-called "sexual perversions" are abortive attempts at love and surrender. This is particularly true in "sadomasochistic" relationships where the inability to voluntarily surrender is dramatically "overcome." In fact many so-called pathological or perverse individuals are closer to understanding the true need for surrender and the willingness to experience it than those considered "normal" by society. The association of pain, bondage or brutality to love is not happenstantial. The facts are that in our culture love has been so intertwined with pain and loss that the so-called "pathological" are often simply expressing the truth of how love really feels. They express a greater degree of honesty than the "average" person who in fact can express nothing about love and surrender.

Many murders and suicides have at their foundation the frustrated *will to surrender.* These violent acts are often attempts to be released from the hardened boundaries of one's private hell—to feel union with the "Other" or the Universe. The assassin of John Lennon is an example of a pathological attempt to merge with the beloved through the act of murder.

Most people feel unable to surrender or be in the presence of someone who is surrendering because of the pain it brings to the surface. They feel the pounding force of life pushing through their skin and they are horrified of losing what sense of autonomy they do have.

Often people who are unable to surrender place themselves in situations which force defeat—a pseudo surrender. Frequently failure of this type is "caused" by the person himself in a desperate attempt to consolidate diffuse feelings of anxiety.

In the afterglow of utter failure they allow themselves to indulge temporarily in an illusion of surrender. They can let go but only in a sham fashion. This provides some sense of relief from the obsessive feeling of having to hold on to their tenuous sense of autonomy.

People who require strict bounds of individuality (guardedness) are usually the least capable of surrendering. Individuals firm within their autonomy are more capable of surrendering. This is identical to the notion that one must actually have a viable ego before one is qualified to lose it.

Those who have had their *primal sense of autonomy* severely impaired by an environment which stressed chronic self-defense in order to maintain their autonomy are all but incapable of surrender. Their sense of autonomy is so fragile, held together by pain and suspicion, that the idea of surrender brings forth intense feelings of shame, anxiety and guilt. Thus, they are incapable of giving love or receiving it. Their habitual defensive posture, learned when they were too vulnerable for differentiated defense, makes it next to impossible for them to drop their guard long enough for love to come in or for love to come out. Ironically, individuals such as these are often those who talk the most about love yet treat their relationships as an endless chain-reaction of negotiations centering around the issue of control.

The entire idea of "control," in this context, contradicts the result people believe "control" might yield—self-mastery. Here control means "control" of anxiety, smallness and the feeling of falling apart which an impaired sense of autonomy has created.

These fears and maneuvers are unfounded and unnecessary, once the person realizes that in reality they can only truly surrender to their Secret Lover. This act of surrender can do nothing but add to one's autonomy and power, but it is important to keep in mind that the benefits brought about by love are always a consequence—a result—of surrender and never the reason for surrendering. The need to surrender is "caused" by life fulfilling itself. Surrendering is a necessary experience for complete living and the *will to surrender* is the ultimate realization of this fact.

Giving love, being tender, showing compassion are as necessary as receiving them: none are a morality. They cannot be legislated. They cannot be enforced. They are a *result*, not a *cause*, of complete surrender.

MAGICK AND MYSTICISM: A FALSE DIVISION

The concept of surrender has become so distorted that many believe that "surrendering" is in opposition to power, sex and self mastery. This is one of the greatest lies.

Exposing this lie is another important point of this book—self mastery *is not possible* without surrender. This issue cannot be overemphasized. Magic and Mysticism—The Will To Self Mastery and The Will To Surrender—are two sides of the same coin. As it is often the case, pseudo-Mystics see Magicians as power hungry individuals uninterested in love. These "mystics" see themselves in the service of love and humanity. In fact their attempt at superiority by appealing to those who can neither love nor use power is proof of their lack of both. They are guilty of the greatest megalomaniacal maneuver—believing that they can love while all the time seeking esteem and power often by the most cowardly means. The "mystic" as described here has shrouded himself in the prophylactic of spiritual pride. You can almost rest assured that in his case—nothing will get in and nothing will get out. As people in the West are so suspicious of Magick little has to be said about the "false" Magician. He is already thought of as an egotist. Yet, it is the Magician more than the Mystic who knows that when power or love are taken to their extreme they become one.

Often this false distinction between magick and mysticism gives rise to strong prejudices against certain practices such as sex magick or the "Tantra of the Left Handed Path." The reason they have such bad reputations is that they teach surrender *and* self mastery. In other words they teach love *and* power and not simply love *or* power. The idea of love *and* power is very disturbing to some people who require external controls to feel safe as well as to those who desire nothing more than to control others.

THE HEART OF THE MASTER

It is more than a colorful figure of speech to say that true surrender takes place in one's heart. The Anahata (Heart) Chakkra of the Hindu system is traditionally opened in the act of divine surrender and the parallel experience in the Western tradition, the Knowledge and Conversation of the Holy Guardian Angel, is an experience of Tiphareth (the Qabalistic Sephirah corresponding to the heart Chakkra).

It is from the Anahata Chakkra, the "home" of the Secret Lover, that each individual finds their own true will and purpose in this life.

In order to know your true will (to be the master), to "light up" with the divine, you must first surrender. The importance of knowing your true will is beautifully conveyed by Sufi Master Hazrat Inayat Khan:

> However unhappy a man may be, the moment he knows the purpose of his life a switch is turned and the light is on... If he has to strive after that purpose all his life, he does not mind so long as he knows what the purpose is. Ten such people have much greater power than a thousand people working from morning till evening not knowing the purpose of their life.

The power of surrender is divinely expressed by describing one of the many samadhic experiences of the great mystic, Sri Ramakrishna:

...He explained that it was impossible to express in language the ecstasy of divine communion when the human soul loses itself in the contemplation of the Deity. Then he looked at some of the faces around him and spoke at length on the indications of character by physiognomy. Every feature of the human face was expressive of some particular trait of character... And so the marvelous monologue went on until the Paramahansa began to speak of the Nirakara (formless Brahman)... He repeated the word Nirakara two or three times and then quietly passed into samadhi, as the diver slips into the fathomless deep.

...We intently watched Ramakrishna Paramahansa's samadhi. The whole body relaxed and then became slightly rigid. There was no twitching of the muscles or nerves, no movement of any limb... The lips were parted in a beatific and indescribable smile, disclosing the gleam of the white teeth. There was something in that wonderful smile which no photograph was ever able to reproduce... As the music swelled in volume the Paramahansa opened his eyes and looked around him as if he were in a strange place. The music stopped. The Paramahansa looked at us and asked. 'Who are these people?' Then he slapped the top of his head vigorously and cried: 'Go down, go down!'

Something similar to this happened to the famed Western Mage Israel Regardie. During the time that Dr. Regardie and Dr. Hyatt were putting the finishing touches on Regardie's *Complete Golden Dawn System of Magic*, (Falcon Press, 1984) he went to his usual chair and had a few cocktails. He excused himself and went to his room. We didn't hear a sound from him for an hour or more. Suddenly, we heard a shout, a yell in Hebrew; he was talking to his Holy Guardian Angel. We looked in on him; he was having a conversation with his Holy Guardian Angel, asking "him" to use him (Regardie) in anyway he saw fit just so long as "he" used him. Regardie was in an ecstatic state. He looked as if he had "left this world," almost angelic. A few moments later he "awoke," and was told what had happened. He replied, in awe and amazement, "I have no memory of it. This is the first time that (it) ever happened to me that way." Later, he would say:

This should happen more often to those in the Western Tradition, but they are too blocked, too much in the head. Instead of working, they talk too much…too worried about attributions…morality…etc.…without living them. (Laughter)

BECOME WHO YOU ARE

THERE ARE NO GUARANTEES

LIE SEVENTEEN

Higher Learning Means Higher Lying

*Truth is one of many propositions used
to hold together a system based on violence.*

It is time to caution the reader—even the idea of individuality is a lie.

One day a middle class intellectual told me that the religion I was born into was a fact. I asked myself, why did he say such a silly thing? Then I remembered that we were both born into the same religion. It served him to hold on to his traditions as it served me to let go of mine. He didn't like my attitude since it violated his notion of tradition. (Tradition is simply the metaphysics of bad habits.) He demanded that I believe in the sanctity of tradition since it gave him a sense of power over my irreverent attitude. More importantly it shored him up in his declining years. He is beginning to worry about how he lived his life.

Truths are simply fictions or metaphors created by tricksters and illusionists to help control the interactions among animals who cannot overcome their desire to herd. *Truth can't exist for those who don't require lies.*

Most herd animals do not even realize that they are herd animals. Most humans don't believe that they have ape bodies. Believing that they are not part of the herd, but individuals, is a "necessary" illusion, which keeps herd animals tame and quiet. This illusion was best served by the notion of democracy—the religion derived from the belief that people are "human" and because they are "human"

133

they "think" rather than react. The only thing unique about most individuals are the statistics used to process them.

Some of you might be familiar with the story of how a Shepherd kept his flock of sheep from running away when they saw the butcher coming. He told each of them privately that they were a lion. When they saw the butcher coming to slaughter a sheep none of them would panic or run. Instead, they would smile peacefully knowing that it wasn't them who the Shepherd would dine on tonight.

BE CAREFUL WHEN SEEKING HELP:
ALL HEALERS ARE HERD ANIMALS

Any person seeking help is always helped back into the herd—although at the time he is being told he is becoming himself. Maybe he is?

Becoming yourself is a most frightening thing and there are few healers who can't be stopped in their tracks by something which truly offends them. When I was in practice I sent devout Christians off to the Jungians. I could not stand their smell. I had a few who ran away as soon as they got a scent of me.

Even Gurus are not concerned with you. Most of them are concerned with supporting their system and expanding their influence and power.

Your worth or value is always determined by how you will benefit the herd. *Thus, every society and every individual is always discriminating in* its *best interests—never yours.* You will always lose even if the other person thinks they are helping you. In the end you must be responsible for yourself even if you do not know who you are. Do not seek to know yourself because there is no self. If you observe yourself you will find this out. If what I said is true did Socrates lie when he said, "*No* thy Self?"

Never be fooled by the herd-animal's mysticism or philosophy—they are always serving themselves first, but they are always disguising their interests by stating that they are serving you. Later they will punish you for what they are doing.

Being morally superior to the normal shepherd, I always serve myself as well as my herd. However, I love no one unconditionally. Those who require unconditional love should worship the dead. *They want Zombie love.* The morality of the herd animal is always incomprehensible to a human being.

Now, think about what I just said: "The morality of the herd animal is always incomprehensible to a human being." Conversely, the "lack of morality," which means unmasking group fictions, horrifies the herd.

A herd animal requires consensus morality because he is not a master—nor can he be satisfied by anyone including himself. The herd animal is *different in kind.*

The danger the herd animal senses when he meets a true individual is real for him and the moralities he requires to contain his neighbor are necessary for him. But remember, necessity is never a virtue.

The herd animal is terrified—but he is horrifying in his pretense of being human. He can and will do anything to keep his safety—to pay the rent. Secretly he is proud of his cowardice—he believes he can survive at any cost—to you. This is the same behavior as the Nazis. The Nazi in the death camp was an ordinary man who was paying his rent and protecting his family. This fact alone horrifies the middle class since it uncovers who they really are—Nazis in the making. It doesn't take much to turn almost anyone into a Nazi.

Morality is nothing more than cocktail glasses clanking at a Christmas party. All "morality" is irresponsible and cowardly. It does not require independent thought or action or responsibility. Herd morality is for cowards.

The weaker we are the more we require someone to remind us that the present has been built on a logical development of "divine purposes" and "natural consequences."

The problem with these abstractions is a simple one—they serve a bad memory? Every great institution is built on someone else's blood. Every college degree is covered with the blood of Indians!

BECOME WHO YOU ARE

THERE ARE NO GUARANTEES

LIE EIGHTEEN

I Had Many Candles But No Cake

When I was twenty one years old I happened to pick up a book by Frederick Nietzsche. I do not even remember which one.

I tried to read Nietzsche but I was put off by his refusal to explain—his refusal to educate—his refusal to let me feel comfortable. He never let me rest. Every time I began to believe I understood something, he stabbed me.

I felt stupid after reading him, but I was attracted to his spirit.

Observing my reactions to his words I immediately knew that most books could be written in less than one page. A lot depended on the reader. Nietzsche continually reminded his readers of the importance of the "right reader."

At that time I needed to be one of the elect and I soon simplified my life and began to study him seriously. Soon I found out that I was better off trying to live Nietzsche as I perceived him at that time. For a period of nine months I tried until I no longer could tolerate my isolation and celibacy.

At that time I did not realize how much Zarathustra liked to dance. I was still a solemn, uptight, serious, academic christian-jew possessed by the values generated by fear and hope. I was still ill with the disease I contracted as a boy. I was too fearful of freedom—I was assured since I was young that real freedom or joy would lead to hell. And the truth is that freedom and joy do lead to hell. Amen!

Nietzsche emphasizes the joy of life when he says,

> ...and I would not know what the spirit of a philosopher might wish more to be than a good dancer. For the dance is his ideal, also his art, and finally also his only piety, his 'service of God.'

After my nine months at "being" Nietzsche I couldn't tolerate my life any longer so I put Nietzsche away and began to live again. I exhausted myself in lust.

I am now forty-nine and I have read most of Nietzsche's books, some as many as six times. I am still not the "right reader," but I can say that he is one of the greatest physiological psychologists that has ever lived.

Nietzsche's work is first a study of the human condition. He observes how men have used concepts and how they react to the concepts they use. In essence he studies and exposes the use of the lie—the metaphysics of meaning. He concludes that error more than truth has served man; this brings him to a temporary nihilistic "conclusion." His position is that man creates meaning and this desire to create meaning is the intrinsic quality which allows man to overcome himself. However, this desire to overcome oneself is not simply a choice, but a "necessity."

Nietzsche's methods are brilliant and to understand his ideas fully you must live them. Thus, Nietzsche cannot be studied successfully. In order to understand Nietzsche you must first apply his methods to yourself.

LET US DANCE WITH JOY
TO THE CURSE OF THE ZOMBIE

Nietzsche's "cure" for the ills of man is a painful one.

What is this "cure?"

The realization that mind creates meaning and then forgets its act of creativity.

Man is a powerful joyous fool. In overcoming himself it appears necessary to forget. In the reality of the moment man is naked. He looks for power over himself and his environment. He is so creative—he invents ideas about himself and nature and bestows upon them an existence independent of himself. He believes his ideas to be true—independent of his need and will to create them. When the forgetting is complete the mortar hardens and he is trapped in the security and horrors of his Gods.

What is the greatness power?
The ability to forget your power.

Man is very creative in the area of metaphysics. He creates beginnings, endings, values, morals, causes, time, justice, things in themselves, laws, order, right, wrong and then forgets that they are his inventions. If he remembered that he invented these "essential" categories of thought his pain would be overwhelming. *The formula is to create, forget and then act as if your "creations" were forced upon you from without—a "necessity."*

Ideas from the sleeping man become "necessities" that both protect and stifle him. No longer living in the moment, having forgotten to dance, he begs and prays to be free again.

What disturbs him most is the idea that there is no one to give him freedom. It is difficult for him to realize that freedom is conveyed by himself right where he *is* now—but this type of freedom is also a horror. It has been said by Herodotus, *"Of all the sorrows that afflict mankind, the bitterest is this, that one should have consciousness of much, but control over nothing."* But, Herodotus is dead. Now it is our time, our turn, to perish through our own excesses.

THE GREATEST SACRAMENT IS ACTION

Nietzsche always asks: who, what and how does an idea benefit? From this he gains an understanding of the type of spirit behind the "curtain" of reason.

Nietzsche's "cure" is to show you, for example, how your pity for others is simply a device to cover up your own vulnerability, superiority and greed. Your sighs and groans of concern are simply your wish for a guarantee. You support weakness because you are too weak to stand the blade of the knife as it passes through you—yet you yearn endlessly to live—to kill the Zombie.

Yet, mankind lives in illusion—the illusion of the shopkeeper. And what is the physiology of this illusion? Forgetfulness—that your instinct to overcome yourself has enslaved you—unless of course you realize that self-overcoming is endless. Security is for the professor's wife and, for her, Nietzsche's idea of living "dangerously" is no where found. Danger is her enemy. Why, because she is all too aware of it.

"BUDDHA AND CHRIST SAY NO TO LIFE"

Nietzsche saw Buddhism as life-negative—A Nay-Sayer to life. Buddhism says no to life by positing Desire as the cause of suffering and then following this up by demonstrating how suffering can be terminated by certain actions and attitudes. Buddha's medicine is the result of Buddha's meditation and understanding. How come so many theories, religions, etc. are based on the fear of suffering? Worse yet, why have so many fallen for it? Is it that life is a dead end? Or has it taken this long until we have the tools to say NO to all limitation. What happens to "all is sorrow" if we become the Gods we imagine?

On the other hand Nietzsche is not concerned with the termination of suffering. In fact, in his discussion of "eternal recurrence," he defines the Yea-Sayer as one who would gladly accept all of life's suffering. This love is demonstrated by vowing to relive life with no changes. The Yea-Sayer says *no* to the cessation of suffering. Nietzsche says it this way:

> Did you ever say Yes to one joy? O my friends, then you said Yes to all woe as well. All things are chained and entwined together, all things are in love, if you ever wanted one moment twice, if you ever said: 'You please me, happiness, instant, moment!' then you wanted everything to return! you wanted everything anew, everything eternal, everything chained, entwined together, everything in love, O that is how you loved the world, you everlasting men, loved it eternally, and for all time: and you say even to woe. 'Go, but return!' For all joy wants — eternity!

Nietzsche regarded Buddhism's development as a symptom of a culture which had reached its peak and was now tired and on its decline. On the contrary Nietzsche's hero was on the assent, willing to endure again and again the pains and joys of existence.

BUDDHA WORKED FOR DOMINO'S— HE DELIVERED

In comparing Buddhism to Christianity, the other Nay-Saying Religion, Nietzsche commented that Buddhism promises little and delivers a lot while Christianity promises a lot and delivers nothing. And what is it that Buddhism delivers? Non-vicarious, individual tranquillity and much more—once we strip away its "seriousness."

In many ways Nietzsche saw Buddhism as a psychotherapy or a physiological cure for the misery of existence. He saw Christianity as a curse. Christianity reflects the quality of life that is desired by its adherents. It values obedience and weakness in this life and revenge and power in the next. Anyone who values Christianity is against life.

DUALISM SPEAKS FOR THE NEED
OF A DANCE PARTNER

An aspect of "yea-saying" is to ask oneself the question—who is the one that is living this life? The answer, of course, is life itself. Duality is simply a game—a creative act—a getting to know—a joyous dance—an interesting lie. Thus, science can never *know*, but simply *describe*. Life can only be "known" when it is no longer living. Zarathustra obeys no rules—for he knows too much. Yet, his knowing is alive.

What is unique to man is The Saying of Yes—in spite of the horror that every Yes is simply a new limitation—a new Zombie that must be killed.

THE EGO AS ZOMBIE

What is this overcoming of the hero, of the self? Not simply the constant struggle to join the herd. Not simply the desires of the shopkeeper and fame-reaper. Those who desire to overcome themselves also wish to overcome the abstract self—the historical self—the ego ideal—the societal self—the definitional self. At the bottom of this overcoming is the life of the happy Hermit. He refuses all definitions—thus—the true criminal. The happy Hermit is the Zombie reborn.

The first overcoming is of the ego because its suffering is very limited and artificial. The surface of the ego is an implant and entirely relational. The suffering of the ego belongs to others. It is the invention of the priests, the politicians, the academics, the psychologists, those who require weakness in order to be "useful."

KILL THE ZOMBIE—BECOME AN ART FORM

Be exactly as you are with all your nonsense—. Realize that misfortune is only an event. There are no guarantees.

Realize that misfortune is only an event—often nothing more than the anticipation of failure—often nothing more than not getting what you think you need—then—.

Once you know this then you will have to face "nothingness"—nihilism—meaninglessness—the limitation of belief, knowledge and your melodies. Learn to call your errors—truth. This has been referred to as the crossing of the Abyss—sometimes called madness.

When what you call yourself dissolves—disappears—the whole will still be the whole—filled with rapturous hideous love. The Zombie of form dies.

All division is a device; simply a way of men working "magic."

Division is the snare—the illusion of suffering itself. Division is also the means from which suffering itself dissolves. But suffering never will dissolve—because men like to divide.

Division allows us to dance ourselves into madness—Oneness.

We heroes set our own snares—and they are same ones set by the slaves—except we have not forgotten—we can now do it consciously because we have destroyed all values, all division—only to create them again—laughing and crying—*alive.*

The spoiled, the weak—those unwilling to exchange value for value—regard Nietzsche's "self-overcoming" as compassionless egotism. They have no right to use such words for they have neither compassion nor ego. They lack both. What they have is need.

In order to understand this negative view we must ask ourselves who holds it. Of course, it is the glorious middle class—those who live in a world of revolving doors.

ONCE YOU FIND THE TRUTH—KILL IT

We ultimately know a person's
true nature by the concepts he employs
to command the unknowable   — CSH

I propose that enough time has been spent on suffering and limitation; instead I posit that man's fear to live in the infinite luxury of life is the prime root of his misery.

Why is man so fearful of abundance? Abundance is unpredictable—out of the ego's control. And what is this ego? It is the fortress by which the whole planet has gone mad. It is man's sense of uniqueness which "paradoxically" always develops in relation to others. In other words, is not every statement a comparative one?

LIMITATION IS SECURITY

Everything a person thinks is relational and every feeling and thought is limited by a matrix of comparative elements.

All descriptions and assertions of individuality are delusional, particularly when placed in a hierarchy of someone else's values.

The fortress ego is built on the shifting sands of division and comparison and thus contradicts the ego's desire for control, uniqueness and independence. This is the great joke played on the ego—the more it tries to be in control the weaker and more dependent it becomes.

Yet, the desire for control is natural and originates from the Self. In fact, how a person attempts to control his life and environment tells us all.

LIMITATION

IS SECURITY

IF YOU KEEP ON DIVIDING
YOU WILL APPROACH 0

The ego as object is one of the crucial factors which leads to conflict, war and violence. The ego is not object, but plasma. If you allow yourself to be without division how can you fight? Yet, to divide, to create conflict through the artifact called consciousness is the first definition of man. Man is the Divider. All division is necessary. Learn to say "so what" to pain. Kill the Zombie.

THE FEAR OF LUXURY

The desire to be an object is the desire to limit the infinite which sooner or later destroys every fortress man builds.

When faced with life's luxury humans invent problems.

Problems provide the opportunity to regain a sense of limitation in face of something which *even God must hide—The Infinite.*

One method used to control the fear of the infinite is to reduce life to forces in opposition.

The belief that opposites really exist and have substance (good/bad, selfish/unselfish, hard/soft, truth/lie, etc.) is an act of creativity to which man will sooner or later plead guilty.

Opposites do not exist independent of the type of mind which requires them nor do they convey valid representations of experience.

For example, pain and pleasure are not opposites. They are intertwined. Pain is a necessary result of the pursuit of pleasure. Or to say it differently, pain and pleasure are necessary conditions of pursuing one's destiny. They are not opposites separated from each other. And even more importantly, to experience either one or both conveys nothing about a morality which might exist in "another world."

Opposites cover up the fact that characteristics exist in degrees: that is, on continua. Continua requires thought.

The way we scale a characteristic determines it's reality for us. For example, masculinity and femininity are not opposites. They do not oppose each other. They are not in conflict. What creates the illusion of conflict and paradox is the way language describes and categorizes differences and similarities. For example, what does the red of an apple mean to a person on the lookout for Reds? Why would a normal person think it paradoxical when a mother kills her child? For the answer to this question look at the phrase "ought to!"

IN THE BEGINNING MAN CREATED PARADOX

Any category, (which is nothing but an arbitrary label to group specific attributes of objects and actions regarded similar or different by selecting and ignoring attributes—qualities and quantities—of the objects or actions being classed) can become partially or wholly identified with the attributes which go into or are excluded in making up a category and vice-versa. Confusing?

For example, murdering your child is excluded from the arbitrary category "parent."

It is not paradoxical if a parent kills it's child. Why? Being a parent first requires that you are a human being which includes the attribute of killing other human beings. In other words, the category "parent" doesn't exclude the reality of first being human. The same holds true for other paradoxes. The mistake of allowing a lower order category on the knowledge tree (parent) from erasing an earlier or more primal category (human) creates paradoxes and priests.

DO NOT BE TAKEN IN BY PARADOXES— ONLY NEWSCASTERS AND OTHER CRIMINALS MAKE THEIR LIVING ON PARADOXES

How could a good Christian cheat us on the used car?

How could the chief of police be taking bribes?

How could a good American betray his country?

He is a minister, how could he beat his wife?

How could the Sunday School teacher have sex with his daughter?

If he loves animals how could he be a research scientist?

How can a doctor cheat his patients?

ADD A FEW OF YOUR OWN..........

IS EVOLUTION
NECESSARY ?

IS EVOLUTION NECESSARY?

More often than not what is "necessary" is nothing but hope.

Let us for a moment explore the *necessary.*

The philosopher Hegel was an expert in *believing* how evolution and the "necessary" emerge.

Hegel posits *spirit,* then he posits *nature* as its opposite, then he posits the concept of *idea* as their synthesis. According to him it is a necessary synthesis. Did Hegel come up with this while standing on his head? Or was Hegel a Zombie.

These neat little packages are sold as Universals, or Laws. Other people oppose these Universals with exceptions which the originator answers by further acts of convolution until a system is built. Now there is something for the academic to "sink" his gums into. Finally, enough people accept these "comings and goings" and the entire "system" becomes ordained by God or becomes Natural Law. The funny thing is, even after the system is shown to be non-sense, academics still study it. They love systems no matter how foolish they are.

What is necessary about Hegel's dance? The answer. A simple mind to believe in a system that conveys power upon its user—what an act of juggling to answer every question with the same answer.

But does this "model of history or progress" really convey anything but Hegel's need to have an "understanding" of change? What good does it do for the mind to call it progress, evolution or...? Might we instead say that Spirit pleases a dying man, Nature pleases a physicist, and Ideas please Hegel?

There is no opposition or conflict or *necessary* evolution except by the way Hegel or, for that matter, anyone has conceptualized the multifaceted, ever changing, intertwined living process. There are simply intertwined differences and similarities. However, these "appearances" are not enough for most men. They are too weak for life's luxury. In the end it is always weakness that demands too much understanding and not enough doing. What makes Karma an explanation? Can it really be an explanation or is it just a wish for some, and a nightmare for others?

WHICH CAME FIRST: THE TOILET OR THE...?

What Is Really Necessary And For Whom?

The conflicted and "necessary" qualities of thinkers such as Hegel provide occupations for priests, politicians, problem solvers, authors, psychologists, philosophers, educators, graduate students and lawyers.

Philosophical problems are created by asking questions which presuppose that an answer is possible in the same format the question is poised. Any question is the result of division; thus any answer must also be a result of division. Language can't convey reality. By necessity any attempt to communicate requires that "things" be left out and "things" be put in. Therefore the answer, like the question, is always a lie.

Philosophical questions are the result of distilling experience into language. By its very nature language doesn't represent the essence of experience, since one effect of language is to structure experience so "it" may be communicated to others. As soon as we reflect upon experience, translate it into words and communicate it to the "other" we have lied. Language always implies equality in experience and understanding. Another great lie?

Once life has been distilled into language we begin to respond to language and not to experience.

Our thinkers have stopped living. They forget that dissecting life into pieces is only a technique, a primitive method for the manipulation of attributes and not a condition of real life. Thus, every teacher is a liar.

All categories are simply whimsical conveniences—filled with joy and horror.

WHAT IS THE PROBLEM?
WE!

THERE IS NO WE
ONLY YOU *AND* ME

Problems do not exist. And for that matter what is a problem? Most often an unfulfilled desire, a discomfort, a contoured whim, an itch. Or is a problem simply complexity—the lack of clarity? But most often a problem is "WE." Thus, every answer is a "WE" answer, a compromise for the herd. Thus, all philosophy soon or later becomes dictatorship—a We, instead of an I.

Lawyers, doctors, academics and most everyone in authority are making decisions for you right now! It is the expert gone mad. Instead of a King we have specialists who at this moment are deciding what's best for you. And you know what? There are millions of people demanding and paying for these services.

ALL PHILOSOPHY EVENTUALLY BECOMES A DICTATORSHIP

WHY IS THERE SUCH A SIMILARITY BETWEEN THE WORDS "COMMUNICATION" AND "COMMON?"

The way we describe "reality" creates problems which demand answers which for the most part create more prob-

lems. We are taught that if we feel discomfort or pain
something must be done and this something must be more
than simply stopping the pain or enduring it—we must find
the culprit known as "The Cause." We must legislate life
out of existence.

We require a nursing home called THE CAUSE.

The "CAUSE" of the dark black school of life is Life
itself, rather than the horrid fact that most people are simply
not up to life.

Humans are so weak that they have given up the luxury
of life for the false security of sorrow. "WE" always equals
security and for the "WE" there are always problems.

Every reaction to pain is simply a statement of whether
one is up to life. Evil is simply the path to the greatest Joy.

The theme of my work is simple—the newman overcomes his conditioning—his canned mind, not as a means
to annihilation but as a means to becoming a newman. The
newman lives from his own experience which is given back
to him by nature when he overcomes his pitiful condition.
Overcoming our origins is the task of each and every
responsible person.

For the dead man—the shopkeeper and his wife—our
hero is a psychopath. How else can a fearful man view a
man who is not worried, not serious, yet sincere and joy-
ful—willing to live with pain and discomfort because it is
his own? How can a "somebody" view a "no-body" who
can dance at his own funeral?

The newman knows that his life is real, because he is real.
His life is real because it expresses his own highest instincts. He is hated because the herd is forced to view their
instincts in comparison to the newman—for what they are:
pathetic.

It has been said by many that to become enlightened
without a morality for the common good is dangerous. The
question remains: dangerous to whom? The answer is sim-

ple—to those who benefit from drowsiness—the manufacturers of the Christmas gift. Enlightenment is dangerous to someone else's tradition. Say no—to tradition. Say yes—to life.

Why are enlightenment and compassion frequently associated? Like the Sufi master who never forgets but always forgives—an enlightened master has compassion while he beats you to death. Compassion for the weak-minded simply means making things "easy," giving them what they need or want. Compassion for the weak is duty, but how can "passion" be dutiful?

These principles apply equally to the Master. He gives you what you need while starving you to death. His compassion is spontaneous—alive and not the kind defined by the weak, the lame, the middle class, the academic and the spoiled.

WHAT DOES A DANCER NEED OF SHOES?

We require a boat only until we have crossed the river. We should not carry our boat with us once we have reached the other side. My experience as a psychotherapist confirms this notion. I made up many stories (boats) for my patients until they were ready to have their skin removed. During their greatest misery I comforted them with lies which gave them hope and meaning. The same lies I used for myself. We were all part of the herd and my license to "steal" was the proof.

They were too far away from the living to face the abyss: that their meanings, their traditions, their "manners" were the cause of their misery and the source of their limitation, yet this form of self-delusion could also be the path to ultimate freedom—only if their misery was viewed as belonging solely to them and they still had enough strength to bear it.

They did not know how to laugh or to dance or even to cry. If the truth be known, I never allowed them to be without their lies. At that time I was blinded by my own needs and self-delusions. Now that I am free from my obsessions there are no patients to treat. This is "nature's way" of saying things are going well for me now. If patients appeared at this point of my life I would know that something had gone wrong. The reader might ask why I say this? The answer is simple; all of psychotherapy is a lie and all psychotherapists are common liars. They are as deluded as their patients, except they believe they see the truth. However, they do help their patients to become complacent in their mediocrity.

BECOME WHO YOU ARE

THERE ARE NO GUARANTEES

LIE NINETEEN

How This Book Will Kill You

*People are at their own evolutionary level
because it is the limit of what
they can tolerate of themselves.*

The essence of this book is your response to the aphorisms at the beginning of this book. This is one of the methods I use to help those who wish to stop being crazy and achieve Madness. To do this, however, you must first recognize exactly how Crazy you are. The Western Koan method—and two others which I present in my other books—make up the general methods incorporating the work of Nietzsche, Buddha and Reich as they flow through me. But remember, I am disloyal to each of these men.

I call these methods "The Foundations Of Transition." The remainder of the work is Nature's. All I can do is help destroy you—to prepare you to receive. The gift that "comes" belongs to no one.

Without further stories, let us get to the Truth.

BECOME WHO YOU ARE

THERE ARE NO GUARANTEES

LIE TWENTY

Every Sentence Is A Death Sentence

Humans are secretly envious of objects.

The great problem for men is to be alive and not die. Change is a horror because it leads to death. And no matter how hard we try to make death a group event it is an Individual Matter.

Someone who is changeable, unpredictable, or unsteady is not only unworthy for the purpose of a loan, but is unworthy as a human being. A good man must be solid as a rock. Thus, every good man is dead. Every man must be made into an object. The fact is that most humans demand it.

We are molded and mold ourselves into our idea of matter. This delusion provides us with a sense of being like objects. Once we believe we can control objects we believe that we have reached their essence and understand them. For a moment we feel safe—then the wall falls down again—where is Humpty Dumpty when there is no-one to see him fall?

The idea of managing individuals as units and numbers is based on the belief in the solidity of objects, consistent behavior and singular identity. These factors alone are insufficient to make the process successful. What is necessary is a desire to herd.

Human society (an illusion) begs for an ordering based on perceptions of outdated and misunderstood laws of physics. Truth is always a function of the needs of the herd. The

157

model of society is the bee-hive. The highest goal for most humans is to live like an insect.

Advances in technology have not been paralleled by human behavior. Technology will not help man to free himself from his cowardice. It will simply build a better prison. Computers used by stupid people "become" stupid computers—much like stupid voters electing stupid leaders.

Sooner or later the planet earth will be a complete asylum unless we begin to say Yes to Life and No to Slavery.

In the end you must create yourself.

BECOME WHO YOU ARE

THERE ARE NO GUARANTEES

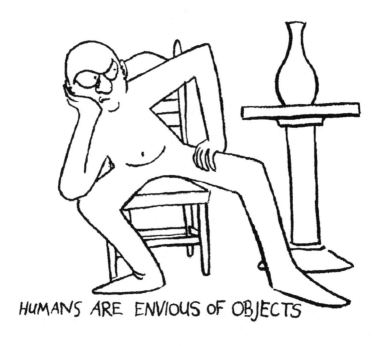

HUMANS ARE ENVIOUS OF OBJECTS

LIE TWENTY-ONE

Bodies In Space Belong To Physics,
Souls In Bodies Belong To The Priests,
And Both Belong To The Politicians

When enough people repress or deny the same quality the attribute appears as either a god or a devil. Thus, we are all responsible for Jesus as well as Hitler. Now, what I just said is truly metaphysics.

Isolating qualities from the whole and giving them independent existence is simply a convenient device that allows us to worship or slaughter each other.

> *Attribute isolation is a primitive technique*
> *of the propagandist, the fascist,*
> *the professor and the priest.*

Separating parts from the whole and then forgetting the whole leads humans to believe that they can destroy "evil" while still having "good."

> *Man is torn between his fear of hell*
> *and his greed for heaven.*

The notion of limitation rests on the desire and terror that the old laws of physics will be suspended. The joke is that Newtonian physics, Plato's caves and Aristotelian logic never hindered a *living* being. They simply used the models to achieve their ends and continued dancing.

> *Our greatest pastime is to create idols*
> *and later destroy them*

> *Most men want to be insects*

159

You cannot avoid the ecstasy-terror of existence no matter how creative you are. There is no end to self-overcoming.

Have you ever heard of Jehovah having a good belly laugh? Or, for that matter, his son? They are miserable creatures and in their misery the flock take refuge.

Never be fooled by a long face or a quick tongue—it doesn't mean *you* know anything.

BECOME WHO YOU ARE

THERE ARE NO GUARANTEES

LIE TWENTY-TWO

Overwhelm Yourself With The Luxury

Every fool thinks he has something to lose. And for that matter every fool *has* something to lose. What is the fool protecting? Why his foolishness, of course—his web of ideas and abstractions which allow him to squelch ecstasy and anxiety. As a matter of intestinal relief I am forced to share my foolishness with others. My books are simply controlled laughter, screams, tears, dancing and joy.

Ortega Gasser says it this way:

> For life is at the start a chaos in which one is lost. The individual suspects this, but he is frightened of finding himself face to face with this terrible reality, and tries to cover it over with a curtain of fantasy, where everything is clear. It does not worry him that his ideas are not true, he uses them as trenches for the defence of his existence, as scarecrows to frighten away reality.

BECOME WHO YOU ARE

THERE ARE NO GUARANTEES

EVERY FOOL
THINKS HE HAS
SOMETHING
TO LOSE

LIE TWENTY-THREE

High Anxiety

Probably the most misunderstood relationship is that between the cognitive process and emotion. While thinking can be enjoyable as an exercise, thinking is *always motivated*. When the motivation is fear-based, as in worry, the emotional component is obvious. Yet, the obvious qualities of anxiety and fear are really not so obvious at all.

Let's say you have two ounces of water in an eight ounce glass. If you add two more ounces of water, the glass will not overflow. But if the glass starts with seven ounces of water in it and you add the same two ounces, the water *will* overflow. If you are prevented from seeing the amount of water in the glass before adding more, you might think that you should have paid attention to what you added.

In reality it is more important that you note was what was in the glass to begin with. In a similar manner, worry, and, for that matter, emotional reactivity has more to do with the *arousal base lines* of the system than with most immediate conditions. Thus, problem solving or issue resolution does not necessarily remove the discomfort a person feels if the arousal base line is continuously high. The reasons for this are many, but one of interest is cognitive processing. When the glass is running over, the person is not able to process the internal state of high arousal. The person is focused on the glass running over. People will—and must—ignore cognitive rational solutions to the specific issue because the mind is over-aroused. Thus, before solutions to perceived problems can be effective, the base level of arousal must be reduced or raised to an appropriate level. In fact many

163

problems are not problems at all—when the baseline arousal is at a low level.

Whatever a particular person's baseline level of charge, it is perceived as both peculiar and normal—for him. That is, if a person is tense and charged most of the time, his sense of tension is felt as "normal"—as *self*. However, the perception of self may change when additional charge is added *and/or* when the charge is reduced. Sometimes a person will not have an altered perception of self when the charge is *increased*, but *will* have an altered sense of self if the charge is *decreased*. Thus, some people feel anxious— feel a sense of impeding disaster—when they *relax*.

When working with people—or yourself—it is important to keep in mind that specific issues feed general charge levels and general charge levels determine the reactions to specific issues. Thus a person can be beset with a multitude of problems for which no set of solutions appear to work. Sometimes this is due to high levels of charge and other times due to the fact that reducing charge creates a type of anxiety (perception of loss of identity) worse than the tension caused by the specific problems.

The autonomic nervous system (ANS) is commonly known as the flight-or-fight bio-survival system. It is designed to help organisms respond rapidly to life threatening situations. The ANS is primarily a non-cognitive system. *Thus simple cognitive intervention has a minimal effect.* So much for positive thinking?

A proneness to high arousal levels is often a necessary condition to the experience of anxiety at a drop of a hat. When there are high levels of arousal, the ability to reduce a specific anxiety is difficult, making many humans poor candidates for normal types of verbal therapies. Anything, and I mean *anything*, which adds to their already high level of "readiness" is experienced as "dangerous" and cause an anxiety reaction. These people may be called chronic or life-style "phobics." The important thing to keep in mind is that it is not the object or situation which frightens them, but their *readiness to be anxious.*

In some people normal defenses to counter anxiety simply do not work. Because of the high levels of arousal, anxiety *itself* is something to fear; the onset of anxiety simply breeds more anxiety. These easily elicited dangers to the self-system create a vicious circle which is frequently difficult to extinguish without the use of drugs or alcohol.

When the autonomic system is inappropriately "taught" to respond to symbols, or it remains active for long periods of time before resolution is allowed, it becomes either hyper-active or dulled. For example a child who must wait three hours for his father to come home to punish him, develops a chronic state of flight/fight reactivity. In addition to this, the fact that children can neither run nor fight back, also develops into an overactive anticipatory fantasy life. The net result is that the ANS becomes "good" at responding to internal cues and images. In other words, the person has strong emotional reactions to thoughts, fantasies and other internal states. When this type of learned reaction is coupled with the child's own hostile fantasies or "taboo" desires, the entire autonomic system begins to feed on itself. The child feels intense anxiety over its own thoughts and feelings. When this child becomes an adult, "little" things can become gigantic issues, and a real crisis can become a catastrophe. The person lives in, and responds to, an over-reactive nervous system (his own reactions) and not to reality. In fact, assessing reality can become a difficult job. People are not who they are, they are "archaic figures" loaded with potential danger.

The interaction of an over-active fantasy life, repressed fears and desires, and an over-reactive nervous system makes a debilitating combination.

When the ANS baseline is high, thoughts about the future easily create "future physiologic" reactions in the present. The person has fight-or-flight reactions to phantoms. Thoughts about the past create a "past physiologic" reaction. The here and now is continually blurred by these "physiologic" prejudices making the individual respond more to these "generated physiologic reactions" than those "caused" by the present. It becomes difficult for individuals to "give" themselves to the moment. Their internal state consists primarily of interactive physiologic reactions to the past and anticipation of the future. For these people the "future," as well as the "past," are always heavily shading the *now*. The present is blurred, confounded and confused.

Each child is born with an autonomic nervous system (ANS) which has a particular hard-wired genetic baseline. Some children respond more heavily to one type of stimulation or bodily condition than another.

Except in rare cases, most children's inborn ANS baseline falls within a healthy and functional range. This baseline can be raised by the circumstances in which a child develops. In other words, since children can neither fight successfully with grownups, nor can they get along successfully without adult assistance (i.e., they cannot flee), an environment which continually threatens them will lead to a very high ANS baseline. Depending on the types and the durations of threats, the ANS baseline can be distorted to such an extent that the child begins to live in a state of chronic preparation. After a period of time this state of chronic guardedness "slips" into the unconscious and is regarded as normal and natural by the person.

The baseline ANS can be elevated at any particular period within the child's development process. If this occurs for a long period of time and over many developmental stages, numerous external and internal cues will be classically and operantly conditioned to this level of arousal. A therapist, Freudian, Behaviorist or whatever, can spend an entire lifetime providing insight and behavioral change with little fundamental change in the Baseline ANS. (BANS).

Not only do particular parental reactions affect BANS, every culture *desires* a particular BANS. A culture such as ours prefers a higher baseline than a traditional Polynesian one.

As a group Americans have a higher baseline than might be desirable as measured by our levels of psychosomatic illness, violence, suicide, child abuse and a myriad of addictions and compulsions.

Regardless of their apparent outward success, children raised in such environments are fundamentally dysfunctional. Their BANS are so high that they are prone to various symptoms as well as to various forms of destructive self-medication.

Not only are they destructive to themselves, they cause unnecessary pain to their loved ones .

It is our view that most forms of self-destructive behavior are primarily attempts to reduce the painful feelings associated with a high BANS, and secondarily to punish or reward the environment or self.

High Autonomic Reactivity (HAR) refers to the increased probability of an undifferentiated non-thinking emotional-thought reaction to a given set of internal and/or external factors. Neither HAR nor its reactions have a present tense survival value, although psycho-physiologically the organism reacts "as if" it does.

HAR acts as an over-readiness to respond. The process is circular and self-perpetuating. Frequently, patients suffering from HAR have been labeled as ultra-sensitive, highly anxious, emotionally flat, depressed, socially incompetent, dull, hostile, unmotivated, fearful, shy, dishonest or manipulative. They are wrapped up in their own feelings, belief systems, childhood training and interpersonal reactions. Because HAR is so high, it is difficult for them to see things for what they are. Everything is highly charged with potential dangers and rewards. Yet, since the origin of HAR is primal, most experiences are a disappointment for them. Nothing is ever enough, nothing truly satisfies. Alcohol, drugs, sex, shopping sprees, and other such "addictions" provide some relief from the pain of being "ever-prepared," but even these forms of self-medication do not relieve the pain of "ever-readiness."

Logic, reason, and insight have little lasting effect. The level of tension is experienced as normal and natural and so is the self-medicating behavior whether it is excessive social contacts, drugs, food, alcohol, or sex compulsions.

Individuals who suffer from HAR are self-medicators and make-up the majority of the population now known as addicts.

HAR is frequently painful and the organism develops defenses to reduce the pain. These defenses are most often developed automatically without critical evaluation or cognitive intervention, and thus continue operating and are automatically reinforcing.

The person experiences HAR reactions as natural and necessary rather than learned and happenstantial. Defense structures fall into two very broad categories known as funneled-confined and barreled-reactive.

Broadly speaking the funneled-confined type tends to restrict input. The barreled-reactive has difficulty in restricting output.

The "automatic and habitual" quality of HAR and its correlated defense structures creates the belief that both HAR level and the defense structures *are the person*. This unfortunate fact makes it particularly difficult to help the patient and gives many clinicians the idea that the patient is "resistant to change." What he is resistant to is losing his sense of himself.

Very high levels of HAR create an internal environment where minor external changes take on significant consequences. Minor and non-threatening situations can be built up into a catastrophe simply because of the high level of HAR. Patients who suffer from this are very difficult to treat, particularly if the therapist pays too much attention to the details of the environmental stimuli and the patient's explanations. In other words, the treating of specific symptoms, complexes, and situations can be next to useless, until the general level of HAR is significantly reduced—although, in practice "life incompetencies" as well as HAR levels are treated at the same time. The difficult issue is getting the co-operation of the patient, since significant baseline changes in the level of HAR create a "rejection phenomenon" similar to organ rejection.

The majority of these HAR's are expressed in social interactions. Thus HAR is an interpersonal event, although the reactions have been internalized into a detailed and elaborate fantasy life.

HAR can inhibit and facilitate learning and learning can reduce or increase HAR.

This implies that learning new behavior can generalize to some degree and reduce HAR, and the learning of new behaviors can be inhibited by HAR.

While this is true, the general state of the person cannot be *significantly* altered by the learning of new behaviors. This makes normal behavioral re-conditioning of habits and self-defeating attitudes difficult at best, since the level of the flight-or-fight response is continuously high. It is difficult to "get a hold of the person" to help him learn. Such people are forever responding to internal cues and fantasies over which the therapist has little or no control.

Conditionability is also a function of autonomic reactivity and is different for various individuals. Some individuals are easier to condition than others. This doesn't imply that re-conditioning cannot alter HAR, but does suggest that careful consideration must be given to the various types and patterns in working out a particular program.

Statistically, HAR is normally distributed; however, the −1.5 standard deviation should be considered the theoretical *ideal*. Average or normal HAR should be considered unhealthy since the population itself is pathological. (We assume the pathology of the masses on the bases of psycho-somatic, stress-related diseases and the frequency and degree of interpersonal and family dysfunction and addictions.) In other words, the typical American family must be regarded as unhealthy, even though it is the statistical mean.

Diagnosis and treatment is a function of contextual defense structure, type, and present level of organization.

Regardless, the goal of therapy is to reduce HAR to acceptable levels without severely disrupting the creative responses of the patient.

BECOME WHO YOU ARE

THERE ARE NO GUARANTEES

LIE TWENTY-FOUR

The Tree Of Lies Revisited

*To Take Joy In Yourself
Is The Greatest Crime.*

INSTRUCTIONS

Go back to Lie Zero. Take the test again. Compare your results.

*Only those
who live from the belly*
CAN TAKE ADVANTAGE OF BOTH ENDS

Some individuals have read these Lies and laughed, others have read them and cried: some have liked a few while others have liked a lot of them. But most individuals have *not* followed the instructions to rank each one. Did you?

If you follow the instructions and come back to your responses in a few days you will begin to see how your reactions have changed. This procedure will provide an opportunity to know yourself better. Your reactions will tell you where you stand and why you stand there.

BECOME WHO YOU ARE

THERE ARE NO GUARANTEES

LIE TWENTY-FIVE

A Dead Man's Journal

THE CATEGORY AS DEATH SENTENCE

Every dream is a neural journal. What follows rolled about in my brain as this book came to an end:

I am a philosopher but I am not a philosopher.
I am a psychologist but I am not a psychologist.
I am a writer but I am not a writer.
I am a man but I am not a man.
I am a liar but I am not a liar.
I am a lover but I am not a lover.
I am a father but I am not a father.
I am a husband but I am not a husband.
I am a businessman but I am not a businessman.
I am a criminal but I am not a criminal.
I am a fool but I am not a fool.
I am an occultist but I am not an occultist.
I am a doctor but I am not a doctor.
I am a religious man but I am not a religious man.
I am a guru but I am not a guru.
I am a weakling but I am not a weakling.
I am responsible but I am not responsible.
I am a devil but I am not a devil.

I am a category(s) only for other people's needs.
Other than this I am nothing.

End of dream.

I have a few enemies who help me stay awake. I find them horrid. They are horrid because I have de-humanized them. Like myself they are corpses. They are filled with self-deceit like all of us, but unlike most of us they believe they are truthful. What follows are the journal entries of one of my most interesting enemies. He recorded these remarks after working with my 250 Lies.

"I can't pretend that I am humble. When I am strong I feel immune from everything. When I am weak I feel vulnerable to everything.

Overall I can only tolerate so much. Some days I can fight like a Lion and not be bothered by the stress. Other days I will give my soul away not to be yelled at. The way I am is neither a virtue or a vice, but something which I and others endure.

Some days I require pity and support and other days I require none at all. No one in the world can provide me with what I need. I can't. No one can. I have a lot of fun...believing that I can fly. When I find myself on the ground I get depressed, angry, that my wings have been clipped.

Some days I make up very good stories. It seems that facts disturb people. When I tell someone that I didn't give them what they wanted because I wasn't interested in their needs today, they flip. When I make up a story they feel better.

I can't stand people who need to extract promises from me because they are anxious. When I am weak I make promises I can barely live up to. At that moment I hate the people who "made" me promise.

I find nagging as a negotiation strategy despicable.

I know how to make every reaction disappear, every mood. I have done it for as long as six months. At one time I achieved true balance. After awhile I found that I was happier bouncing off ceilings and walls.

I am understanding and intolerant. I am a great joy and a pain in the ass. Very few people can tolerate my penetrating nature. I seem to see through words but I am blinded by beauty. The only victories which I claim are those few over myself.

I have contempt for humble people who have something to say. Humble people should remain silent.

When I feel humble I am feeling vulnerable and weak. I don't think the way I live is special or superior to anyone else's bad habits. I resent people who write so small that you're forced to use a magnifying glass to read their writing. I hate pull over faded sweaters and think the 50's were a horror.

I don't like loud sounds or being yelled at.

I think that nothing is good enough for me. When I reflect on this I feel embarrassed.

I know that everything great was built on violence and blood. I enjoy telling graduates of prestigious Universities that their great School is legitimate because it is built on the skeletons of dead Indians.

Legitimacy is always necessary after a blood bath.

Smugness and humbleness go together for most men. I dislike having dinner with academic types, particularly when they are wearing their sweaters.

I feel that the human condition is absurd. What makes it tolerable for me is men who make something out of it— heroes. Sad to say I am not a hero for myself. I think that is impossible for anyone who lives in a skin. It's what you do in spite of the existential condition that makes life interesting for yourself.

If nature has a plan I don't know what it is. I mistrust anyone who thinks they know nature's plan. There is no such thing as natural law. Men have laws; nature at best has "consequences."

I enjoy watching people who believe in the system losing what they value most. I get a thrill from true believers finding out that life doesn't care what they believe.

I think that women who act as if their vulnerability to a male's violence gives them a sense of moral superiority are fools. Any woman who lives with a violent man is a coward.

I enjoy watching self-righteous people. Their sense of moral superiority is fascinating.

I like the feeling of death close by—unless it's too close.

Very few people are capable of "seeing" when they are talking.

I dislike being rejected because I do not live up to someone else's desires, yet I reject people because they don't live up to mine.

I am very unaccepting of roles and appearances.

I laugh a lot.

I am basically kind, but unfriendly.

I do not have view points, I am my view points.

I am very moody and changeable. I soar the heights and sink to the depths.

I like to be held and hold others I love. I don't like people touching me unless they love me.

I have learned a lot from other people but had only one true teacher-friend.

I'm not impressed by people who have to die. That's only a half-truth. I am impressed by people who make things happen. Yet, I know in the silence of the moment each person is naked and vulnerable.

Protecting my self-image has cost me more than anything else.

It is amazing how powerful laughter is.

The power of social rejection and ridicule is more powerful than violence. I am forever amazed at its power.

Most everyone is hiding the fact that they are the center of the world. The reason they hide this fact is because somehow they know that everyone else feels that way too. What is fascinating about people is how they go about hiding their secrets and how they go about exposing them.

The most self-centered person is always the one who is looking down at his shoes when he walks. The more horrible a person feels about themselves the more self-centered they are. What their depression reveals is the refusal to admit that in the end they are not alone in their delusions. Everyone is struggling with the same issues in one form or another.

Everyone I meet offends me, for he too is a center and forever reminds me how I hold on to my delusions to make "me work."

All of what I have just said are simply experiences, they are not the way I live or even think. But they are reflections, moods, thoughts, experiences, hopes and fears."

Well, I hope you are not depressed by these journal entries. As I said, I need enemies and who better than myself to wrestle with.

BECOME WHO YOU ARE

THERE ARE NO GUARANTEES

LIE TWENTY-SIX

Violence

*The greatest cause of violence is the refusal
to label violent behavior violent.*

All human behavior is violent.

By violence I mean, the act of getting more, the act of collecting space, the act of competing and negotiating, the act of living itself. Even digestion is violent.

Violence, the killing and transforming of energy sources is not a moral concept but a biological and psychological one. Making violence moral simply politicizes the making of weak, sick slaves. It is time that some of us have the stomach to face up to what we are really doing. In reality all living things are doing the same thing—living off of other living things.

What makes humans different and possibly more dangerous is that we lie about it. Remember lies are useful as well as dangerous. We must ask ourselves who requires what set of lies to function. The more complex and confusing the standards which motivate lying the more cowardly (though possibly) creative the liar.

Civilization and the social contract have at their base the exchange of personal violence for collective violence repackaged as deception.

We agree to let other people be violent for us. The use of the word violence in this context is usually reserved for physical violence against other people. The social contract exchanges the "right" of physical violence of the individual, for collective violence known as "justice."

179

In other words, the concept of justice is "necessary" for the practice of collective violence. It removes the guilt and shame from the individual for not "fighting" his own battles and "justifies" his cowardly and sneaky behavior.

It is claimed by those who benefit most from the "social contract" that one of it purposes is to protect the weak from being exploited by the strong. This is a gross deception. The truly strong find it inefficient to exploit weak individuals by physical violence. Direct exploitation runs a risk of revolt and a reduction in gross profits. The social contract allows the strong to exploit the weak without fear of their own blood being shed. Blood is too expensive for the strong. Insurance policies are cheaper and more profitable.

When physical violence is seen as necessary and the goal is reached, the first act of the victor is to outlaw the use of further physical violence. Like all governments, America was founded on violence and has survived on violence. Yet when individuals act violently to assure their existence they are beaten-up by the system. Then the leaders tell the victims that violence is not a solution to their problems.

The social contract allows the development of a class of individuals which act as a protective buffer between the upper and lower classes. This is the *middle* class. The worst of these is the upper-middle class.

This subgroup is intellectual, cowardly and inflated, and prefers lawyers and slight of hand to guns. They use law to steal from each other. They make the weaker minded impotent by using metaphysical concepts such as right and wrong, good and bad, moral and immoral. They use law to commit murder, they use law to steal and they use law to make impotent those who might rise against them. This they call education. What they want is "more." Too much competition is dangerous so they create more laws and regulations making it more difficult to compete with them. Law is the ultimate act of camouflage.

The upper-middle class (UMC) label these laws as *necessary* to protect weaker people from being exploited. This assertion is the bait which most everyone can agree with because everyone from time to time feels weak and dependent. Boiled down, the whole procedure is a "club" with various levels of initiation.

They thrive on regulatory agencies who are staffed by lesser (middle and lower-middle class) individuals who have nothing to lose if their regulation fails.

The intermediate class, like all groups, are allowed—up to a point—to steal, rob and murder for profit, much like the strong. The only differences are that they do it on a small scale and the label it differently. For the doctor and lawyer it is called "service." For the shopkeeper it is called "merchandising." Whatever it is called, it is violence.

"More" is what is wanted. Nothing more or nothing less. "More" is the answer. The nice thing about this plan is that everyone is doing it to everyone else. There are no honest men. Everyone is a thief. To make such harsh statements as this will not make me popular; no one likes to be stripped of his camouflage.

It is important to note that all that I have said is true only if we assume that the lies of the propagandists are true. That is the idea of an honest man, a man of virtue, etc. as described by the Bible: the lawyer and the educationist. As the "necessity" of these values—their "other-worldly" quality are simply assumptions, or whims—we are forced to ask the horrible question: "who do these values serve?"

These values, like any other values, are "unessential" in their content. Thus we are left with a relativistic picture making the moral tone of my discussion simply misleading. There are no thieves—dishonest men—*a priori*.

They only become so within a system of relativistic values which change as the wind blows. But, the secret to all this is to make these relativistic values "necessary" for life to continue—in other words, necessary for survival. We are then faced with the question: whose survival?

Forced now to ask the question, "What *is* necessary for survival?" I reply, "For whom?" For a man without a pan-

creas insulin is necessary. For a man without lungs an artificial breathing device is necessary. Yet, the question I have
asked concerning survival is misleading. A more interesting
question is "What is necessary for life to expand" since, as
we said earlier, man is interested in "more" and not simply
in staying alive like other animals. What is "necessary" for
"more?" For one thing, *time*. "More" is also self-defined.
For one man "more" can mean "more" lovers, for another
"more" can be safety. I knew one fellow who spent his
entire life figuring out ways not to be hurt by other people.
No matter what plan he came up with he always found
"more" ways to improve it until he reached a point when he
figured out that he couldn't afford the money it would
require to build his ultimate fortress.

Man survives to make "more." If we can, for a moment,
assume this to be true, the foundation of life itself is a value
system which might have its basis in the nature of man
himself and not in other worldliness. As men are different,
the "mores" which they desire are different in kind and in
degree. Yet, there is conflict and the purpose of civilization
is to provide bloodless means of resolving these conflicts
and allow for the creation of "more." What I am positing is
that the means have become "more" important, "more"
essential than what they are supposed to resolve. And this is
something we would expect from the "more" hypothesis.
However, what we observe is that the "essential and more"
of civilization is now creating "less," and the only way
around the "less" is to violate the "more" factor of civilization. In other words we have a means-ends reversal. If the
end was "more" the means to accomplishing "more" is
creating "less." Thus, the means for "more" is restriction
and not freedom. What is wanted is "more" control. "More"
control can only occur by reducing variability (individual
differences). A "golden mean" is created, allowing for
"more" control. This is created by law, a three letter word
for violence. The purpose of law is first and foremost to
prevent those in power from losing it. All other explana-

tions are propaganda, albeit necessary propaganda for those who require massive amounts of illusions. But, what about those who require less illusion and more freedom? This desire is the beginning of the underground, a world not seen, but felt. It keeps the upper-lower class, the entire middle class, the lower-upper class, the middle-upper class, and some of the upper-upper class nervous. Those who really understand the problem of information and wealth are fortified by the underground; they know that information, used properly, creates wealth and that true wealth creates information. The street poor understand this too, but are unable to apply it beyond certain limited situations. They know what it means to live off of refuse. They know what it means to kill or be killed. But is this all that civilization promises? Less painful and horrifying ways of dying and having unused goods? No. Civilization means safety for those who require it and from our analysis they seem to far outweigh the ones who prefer freedom and "more." The majority of the population demands "more" without payment. And what is the payment? The possibility of having "less." The majority of the population requires more safety without the concern of price.

LIES BUILT UPON LIES BUILT UPON MORE LIES

Psychoanalysis is a prime example of lies built upon lies. A behaviorist can remove a phobia in a few months for $1000. A psychoanalyst cannot, as a rule, remove the same phobia in five years for a cost of $50,000. Yet, psychoanalysis is allowed to be labeled a treatment. Now, a treatment which fails almost consistently should not be called a treatment. Yet there it is. It takes years of training to do nothing but provide an environment where change takes place simply because of time and a change of "scenery."

In fact, many psychoanalysts understand this and justify their "profession" by calling it "research" into how the mind works. Now is the patient interested in paying for this? Of course not. There is little scientific evidence available to show that the "treatment" called psychoanalysis is any better than "maturation" or time itself. Psychoanalysis is simply a holding intervention at best. To call it treatment is like calling blood-letting a treatment for fever when an antibiotic is cheaper and more effective.

Psychoanalysis is safe because it can do little harm to a person except separate him from his money and prevent him from getting a treatment which might be of value. The labels make it both attractive and workable. Of course, psychoanalysts have much to say about more effective treatments. They say it is not a cure and new symptoms will occur. What is the evidence for this claim? "Freud or so and so said it." And what is their evidence? Well?

Who *are* these psychoanalysts, be they Freudians or Jungians or whatever? They are the upper-middle class, those who get "more" by acts of deception. Their hands are clean. There is no blood. As laws create criminals, the profession of psychoanalysis creates psychopathology and patients—eternal patients—some staying in "treatment" for as long as 20 years. Yet, this form of violence is done legally and morally, as long as the Doctor is qualified by some qualifying agency. And what qualifies the qualifying agency? Law, of course. Yet, where did the law come from? From those who had the power to enforce their will upon others and then outlaw the possibility of someone doing the same to them.

Thus physical violence is filtered through enough labels and procedures that it no longer appears as violence. The longer an institution exists the further it is separated from the blood it shed to establish itself, the more "legitimate" it appears to its "graduates" and to the public. Time not only heals wounds, it hides the blood.

BECOME WHO YOU ARE

THERE ARE NO GUARANTEES

LIES BUILT UPON LIES
BUILT UPON MORE LIES

LIE TWENTY-SEVEN

The Information Trap— Gun-Fight At The O.K. Corral

Do not be fooled by technology or the information explosion. Insects do what insects do. They apply everything to their limited perspectives and goals. Thus information and technology alone are not enough to free man from his enslavement.

In fact slavery has *increased* since the days of the Wild Wild West. Proportionally, more people had freedom then than now. No one had to carry holographic computer encoded driver licenses with them. If people didn't like an area or violated a law they simply moved on. Now everyone is kept track of. True, a few computer whiz kids can outsmart the State's computers, but when you compare the equipment the State has with the equipment any one individual has, the difference is overwhelming. Compare this to the outlaw-rebel of 100 years ago. The town sheriff and the outlaw were more or less evenly matched.

Today, more and more people are becoming outlaws—not because they want to—but because they are made to by the State's creation of more and more laws. Today, more than ever, your body is owned by the State. Every one of us is considered a "Human Resource."

We all know that resources are owned and the owner has the right to do what he will with his resources. As humans owned by the State this entails, among other things, being kept track of. With credit cards, your purchases, *and your location,* can be tracked instantly; cash will all but disappear in the near future. As always there will be "good" reasons for this, but as always the result is the same. More and more slavery.

The process of enslavement, however, can only continue up to a point, when the system collapses of its own weight. If humans are property of the State, the State becomes obliged to care for them. As the burden of this becomes more pronounced and as individuals demand more security, the State *of necessity* must surrender its control or perish. You can see how this process occurs in the demise of the U.S.S.R. and in other places.

As the State raises more and more funds to fulfill its role as the *Ultimate Parent,* its children will become more and more dissatisfied with the little bit that is returned. Since the parent is in severe debt it can only remain in its role by printing money or by cutting costs or by raising taxes. All these methods will lead to disaster. There is no need for riots or revolution since the burden of debt itself will cause the State to "get out of the child rearing business." Instead the State will begin to spend money on frontiers. With new frontiers there is hope for people to have a life of their own again. Those willing to take the risks will leave and those who require parenting will stay behind. This is so ironically expressed in the phrase, "The meek shall inherit the earth." This will be the legacy of the insect. He will have his hive. But those of us who wish to suffer the consequences of our own "mistakes" and triumphs will be free to leave, not because of the State's virtues but because of its fears.

Although technology has created more leisure, it has also created more docility and slavery. The collision between insectoid values and the human forebrain has so far been won by the insects. Every new device remains in the service of the hive. This is so because nothing has been created which puts an end to fear and trembling. Death has not been conquered. When death *is* conquered (which in my view will happen within fifty years), a tremendous change will take place. Nothing will remain the same. Our whole archaic system will collapse—and this includes the atomization of the nuclear family. This sacred cow, this filthy evil, responsible for so much human misery will find its place along side the dinosaur in the Museum of Natural History.

Humans will have the opportunity to explore the vastness of the Universe, not in the role of the slave, but as the Gods we imagine. With new frontiers there is adventure and with adventure there are possibilities which only science fiction appreciates. The planet Earth is only a way-station floating in space. This era of slavery will have passed and those of us with vision and fortitude will be remembered as the first "men" of tomorrow.

BECOME WHO YOU ARE

THERE ARE NO GUARANTEES

LIE TWENTY-EIGHT

The Nature Of The Beast

I am not going to pull any punches here. The nature of the beast is quite depressing. For example, the fact that early childhood training affects the organism to the degree it does argues for a very primitive species. Regardless of the cortical processes or "consciousness," early childhood trauma, modeling, beliefs and training stay with most people until they die. This argues for a tribal form of intelligence; early programming remains with the organism almost regardless of cortical feedback.

"Humans" are more ape-like than they would like to believe. For the most part they do not *think* but rather— *have thoughts*. While they use the technique of logic they are not rational. Not only do they not serve the interests of the planet, they do not even serve their own interests. Their vision of the whole is extremely limited. Each is hard-wired to believe that his or her experiences are primary and "necessary." The organism views happenstance as a necessity. It is difficult for it to view its learning as accidental.

Each organism is fundamentally set to re-produce itself, dedicating most of its life to this function. Each believes that it is civilized because it wears clothes, has shelter, drives a car and can talk. Each believes that it has free-will when more often than not it is responding to limited and distorted hedonic and biological needs. Almost every member of the species does the same thing within a set limited range. While cultural differences seem profound to some, they are nothing more than different styles of doing

191

the same thing. Cultural differences are primarily due to geography, genetics and experience.

To sum it up the human being is not quite so human after all, but is an animal with speech, larger cortex, etc. What makes the human being dangerous to itself and the planet is that it can only compare itself to apes and "gods." Thus its perspective is extremely limited. It has a difficult time changing itself regardless of all the technological advances it has made. In my view these "advances" are minimal and late in coming. Very little has been done to change man's out-of-control breeding patterns to fit with developmental and planetary goals. There is very little brain technology to develop the cortex, to aid in re-programming the brain and overcome the early imprinting and conditioning of the lower brains.

The so-called educational system is a joke. The majority of Ph.D's. can neither think nor apply their knowledge.

The beast is insecure, frightened and aggressive. It is dangerous to itself, the gene pool, and the planet. I view the human as a developing system with the potential to become more than what it currently is. I only see this potential as an *opportunity*—I do not view a *potential* as a *necessity*. In other words, the human being is a question mark. Neither optimism nor pessimism can account for the energy and force required to enhance human potential. Courage, power, intelligence and hard work are necessary. These attributes alone can overcome the limitations of gravity, stupidity and death. I repeat the quote from Dr. Robert Lindner. As you read, replace the word "psychotherapy" with "brain-technologies" and replace the word "recovery" with "aiding of individuals and groups." If I am accused of being optimistic because I have utilized this quote I can only say that neither optimism nor pessimism has made a rose grow. My point of view comes from my inability to tolerate my own energy in a highly restrictive world.

"...the various psychotherapies have as their job the recovery
of individuals and groups for evolution so that those whose

lives would otherwise be wasted can also contribute toward the same end: the coming glorious breakthrough into...What?"

BECOME WHO YOU ARE

THE LIGHT OF THE WORLD

APPENDICES

POWER IN THE WORLD

What's Left Over?
How Much Fun And Status Can You Have?

BY NICHOLAS THARCHER

All your life you've been told that if you "work hard" you will "succeed"—you will have "money and power." Do you really believe that if you work hard you will succeed? "Of course not," you say, "any fool knows that you can work as hard as you like at street sweeping and all you get is a clean street." And, of course, you are right. Working hard, by itself, is not sufficient and may not even be necessary. So now we ask: what *can* you have by trying to live out the "American dream?"[1] Is it possible for you to be "useful and harmless" and still have any fun, status and power? Let's see.[2]

So things don't get too complicated, we'll make a few simplifying assumptions. (As honest men, we cannot help but to reveal assumptions; we abhor "assertions" made under the guise of "truth." Another lie?)

The income figures are deliberately at the high end of "middle-" to "upper-middle class." This is not simply to make our case stronger (it does), but because we assume

---

[1] This chapter is strictly for those of you in, or aspiring to be in, the "middle class." If you are truly poor you already know the lie of the "American dream"; and if you are truly wealthy, you don't care.

[2] These words are being written in 1992 using U.S. dollar income and expense figures. If our expectations of financial conditions in the next few years come to pass, readers in the future may find these numbers "quaint."

that if you are at all interested in fun, status, and power and have an average dose of creativity and smarts, you probably can find a way to earn at least this much. The income and expense figures are more or less typical for a middle class neighborhood around a large city in the U.S., such as Los Angeles or Chicago.

So let's say you have "worked hard" and, in 1992, you are thirty years old and single with a Gross Annual Income of $55,000.[1]

That gross amount shrinks pretty quickly through the magic of "deductions." There are deductions for federal income taxes, usually deductions for state income taxes, and sometimes deductions for city income taxes; there are deductions for social security taxes, disability taxes, etc., etc. And there may be more deductions for health insurance, dental insurance, disability insurance, pension plans and more. The list can seem staggering. (And, as such, most people simply ignore them all together. "Oh yeah, Joe, I got a *good* job. *I* make $55K!" Sure you do.)

So how much do you have left after all of these "deductions?" Maybe $35,000 for the year—$2916 each month.

Now you need to live on this. We'll be fairly frugal here. After all, with an income of $55,000 you're not "rich." (Or are you? According to the federal income tax rate structure, a single person making this much is getting pretty close to "rich." Remember that the next time some politician talks about "soaking the rich"; he may be talking about *you*.)

---

[1] How you quote your income tells people your "class." "Blue collar workers" quote an hourly wage; lower level "white collar workers" quote monthly gross and middle/upper level "white collar" types quote annual income. "Professionals" (e.g., shrinks, doctors, and lawyers) quote annual income to non-professionals and hourly to each other and to customers (especially true for shrinks and lawyers). Truly wealthy people do not deal in any of these terms and use a *qualitative* vocabulary—e.g., "I'm comfortable." Remember this the next time you want to give someone a particular impression of your economic class.

Here's a monthly budget for your basic needs:

Rent $700
  (A modest one bedroom apartment in Los Angeles)
Car Payment   300
  (Car prices range from $8,000 for an "econobox" to $200,000 or so for an "exotic" sports car. We'll pick an "average" car: cost about $17,000, a down payment of $3000, and financed over 5 years.)
Insurance   150
  (For the car. Add more if you carry other insurance.)
Fuel   50
Repairs   50
Food   300
Utilities   50
Phone   60
Clothing   100
Dry Cleaning   100
  (Not cheap to keep an office job, is it?)
Medical   50
  (Not everything is covered by insurance.)
Miscellaneous Loans 200
  (Furniture, stereo etc.)

Total $2,110

You are left with $806 a month—$9,672 for the year. This is called "disposable income."

What kind of power, security, fun or status can you have for $9,672.

You could save it all, but that gives you a monk's life with no fun or status until later—you hope. Most of us need *some* enjoyment now. So let's say you spend some of it on current pleasures:

One dinner at a better than average restaurant for two each month is $100.

Two cheap dates each month is $50 (A movie ticket is $7.50; a concert ticket is *lots* more.)

So, annually, you spend $1,800 on modest entertainment.

Take a vacation: 2 weeks at $2,500

Maybe you support some causes and/or people that you care for and give some modest gifts over the year: $500

Disposable income left: $4,872

By the time we get to age 30 most people feel a need to "provide for the future." So you might want to save some of this for your future security.

Let's say you save $3,000 this year. (If you continue to do this for the next thirty-five years, how much will you have at your "retirement?" We'll assume an 8% return, a 4% inflation rate and *no* taxes on the income from these investments. After taking out inflation your gross return is 4%. So how much do you have at age 65?

Just over $228,000.

Not much of a retirement fund is it? (If we didn't factor out inflation, the number is about $573,000. Sounds better, doesn't it?)

Now, if you don't take out any principal, your annual income will be about $9,300—less taxes. On the other hand, if you set it up as an annuity for ten years, you can get $28,100 per year—less taxes. Have fun in your old age. Live it up.

("What about Social Security," you ask? Don't ask. We doubt there will be much for you thirty-five years from now. Check it out for yourself.)

When the year is done, you've lived modestly, had a little fun and made some provision for the future. What's left? $1,872.

What kind of status or power or fun can you have with that?

What to do?

Well, you *might* appeal to the Great Goddess Hope.

Go on, take some chances. Go to Las Vegas. Play the commodities markets for a few days. Now you probably have $0 left. No good.

Aha! How about getting married! Now you have the possibility of two incomes and the entertainment of the relationship besides! So let's find someone you can stand being around for more than five minutes and who's also interested in supporting your ideals of fun and power.

Let's say that each of you earns a gross of $55,000. Couple's gross is $110,000. (Wow, you're *rich*!!)

Monthly net income: $2,916 x 2 = $5,832 (Taxes and other deductions are about the same).

Here are your expenses:

Rent	$900	(You do need a bigger place.)
Two Car Payments	500	(One's a cheaper car)
Car Insurance	250	
Fuel	100	
Car Repairs	100	
Food	500	
Utilities	70	
Phone	120	
Dry Cleaning	200	
Clothing	200	
Medical	100	
Miscellaneous Loans	300	
Total	$3,340	

Disposable income: $2,492 per month x 12 = $29,904 for the year. Take out:

Entertainment	$3,000
Vacation	$5,000
Retirement funds	$6,000
Gifts	$1,000

And that leaves $14,904 disposable. Looking better. Now you can start feeding some of your status needs.

What to do? What to do? Do you get something *right now* or save up and get something more substantial later? What are some of your options? How satisfying will each of them be for you?

Right now you can buy, for cash, a couple of medium priced Rolex watches. You probably won't be able to wear the watch very much these days; most people with Rolexes never wear them for fear of being robbed.

How about "upscaling" the cars? (I just *love* Yuppie-talk?)

You could trade in your inexpensive, low-status cars for a high status matched pair of Mercedes Benz's, at a total cost of about $100,000. You'll need a down payment of $20,000 (you'll manage that "somehow") and payments of about $1,400 a month (for the next seven years). If you're a car buff, you might get a lot of satisfaction from this choice; otherwise, like most people, the excitement will wear off years before the payments do.

What else might you do? You're still living in a modest no-status apartment. How about buying a house! Isn't that the key to the American Dream? A house could be just the ticket to status. How much money do you need? For a slightly better than average house in Los Angeles figure a price of $350,000. (Currently there's a lot of variation in the cost of the same house in various parts of the U.S. In rural areas, the same price could get you a near mansion.) You'll need $70,000 for a 20% down payment plus "closing costs." To cover that you'll need to save all of your disposable income for about the next four years.[1]

(How much will you need each month to pay for this house? Assuming a 9% mortgage for thirty years your

---

[1] Of course, all of this is highly simplified. You might borrow the down payment from your parents. You might qualify for special financing. You might find a low- or no-down payment "deal" with owner financing. Of course, some of these options could mean higher monthly payments, too.

payments will be about $2,250 a month—$27,000 per year. You'll have the $14,904 plus the rent of $10,800 you're currently spending. Not quite enough, but with your hoped-for better-than-average salary raises over the next four years, plus the additional income tax deduction from the mortgage interest payments, you should be able to scrape by. Property taxes, repairs and insurance will strain the budget a bit. And, of course, you'll need new furniture and carpeting and drapes. But don't dwell on those costs too much; you might lose hope and get depressed. Instead look forward to the joys of being a *homeowner*.)

You are now 34 years old.

You have your dream house and spend your weekends and holidays and vacations gardening and mowing and fixing and improving. You're saving up for the room additions and kitchen renovations and maybe a pool.

You're getting a lot of action! You have a sense of purpose and maybe even a little sense of meaning. But don't look too closely at that end of it. Because soon you'll feel the same emptiness you've felt after the shine has worn off any new toy. Toys may give you some fleeting status, but where's the *power*?

Well, there's still something left that can give you an enormous sense of meaning and a tremendous feeling of power for the rest of your life. What's that? Children, of course. Think of it! Eighteen or more years of every kind of decision and confrontation and moralism. Diapers, drugs, school, sex, clothes, music, doctors, dentists. And in your "golden years" you can look forward to grandchildren. Maybe even great grandchildren. Immortality!

"Wait a minute, wait a minute," you say. "What about my work. Don't I get any satisfaction or status or power from *that*?"

Well, if you are the average lower- or middle-class "worker," no, you don't get much of anything from your work except a paycheck. Look at your parents, look at your colleagues and friends. Do *they* wake up each morning *yearning* to work? Do you? What kind of joy or meaning can you get from working on an assembly line or behind a desk? For most people, work is slavery—figuratively and *literally*. What kind of power and status can a slave have?

If you *do* get close to any real power, there's a neverending parade of sharks and parasites waiting to take it from you. There are those who already have power; they see you as a threat to *their* power. On the other hand, there are the inadequate and incompetent who claim anything they "need" as theirs, *by right*; and there are plenty of guns—governmental and theological—to back up their whining.

So this is life—*life as you've been trained to live it*. Your masters demand that, like any good slave, you must feel "gratitude" for the "privilege" of having been born. They "teach" you how to talk and how to eat, when to piss and where to shit. They force you to go to a "school" where authoritarian strangers indoctrinate you in "getting along." When you have been properly "socialized," it's time for you to work, and to breed. If your masters have done their jobs properly, they can count on you to train *your* offspring to do it *all over again*—and then it's time for you to get out of the way and die.

Any variation from the program is rebellious, adolescent and psychopathic.

If you want *real* power, you have to find another way. Look at those who already *have* power. Learn from them. Do what they do. Live off the fictions of others. Become a politician.[1]

BECOME WHO YOU ARE
THERE ARE NO GUARANTEES

---

[1] Better yet, read Christopher Hyatt's *The Psychopath's Bible: For the Extreme Individual* (New Falcon Publications, 2003) and learn...

SOME METHODS OF CREATION

BY JAMES D. NEWMAN

Humanity's most delightful potency is that of the creative response. We are born with the ability to look upon a blank page and fill it with patterns from our imaginations, or to look upon existing patterns and imagine new ways in which they can be combined and interpreted. Out of fear and shame, many adults restrict their creative response, and insist upon the worship of pre-existing forms, naming them "God," and "Reality." In this worship of images they lose touch with reality's dynamic aspect, both as expressed through themselves, and through the world around them. They only see what is and refuse what is coming to be.

Two powerful methods of breaking down the worship of false gods are the acquisition of new information and the randomization of existing information. The check on this process, necessary to prevent dynamism from disintegrating into chaos, is productive creative work expressed into the world, and honest assessment of, but not surrender to, the world's feedback. By itself, the worship of the new leads easily into dilettantism; the worship of randomization leads into obscurity; and the worship of feedback leads to slavery to popular opinion. All three excesses are shallow; all three fail the creative spirit.

The process described in this essay combines gathering, randomizing, and feedback processing—all under the direction of the creative identity—*your* discretion, *your* decision. It is an exploration, designed to break down the fear of new information, the undue respect given to established systems, and the fear of the world's response to your individual creative endeavor. It is not a formula for the creation of art. It is an exercise for the exploration of the extension of the creative identity. Each phase of the overall exercise has advanced workings for further development. A really creative person should be able to capture the feel and sense of these exercises and apply them to other kinds of expression and work. I invite you to push beyond!

PHASE I

Gathering Dead Wood

a) Get a journal. (This simple step separates magicians from book collectors and dilettantes.)

b) Write two pages on each of the following (be totally uncritical):

1) I believe that...
2) The person I hate the most is...
3) My favorite thing about myself is...
4) The worst thing about the world is...
5) The most interesting sexual game is...

These exercises are for you, not for your tenth grade English teacher, your hyper-critical best friend, or any other self-appointed god of good writing. Ignore any internalized rules: originality, grammar, coolness, morality, etc. You are not writing poetry; you are not creating art. You are gathering dead wood with which to build a fire. Dead wood need not be pretty or original, it just needs to burn.

Advanced Exercise

At the end of each day, write a brief (three to five page) essay in your journal with the dead wood rules (i.e., no attention whatsoever to rules) on one of the following premises:

a) The strongest emotion I felt today and the circumstances which gave rise to it.

b) A passage selected randomly from my least favorite book.

c) My most fulfilling daydream/fantasy and the situation immediately around me when I was having it.

d) What would I do if I had sufficient power to change one thing about the world finally and absolutely, and why.

If it helps you to get the ball rolling, start the exercise by visualizing your harshest critic clearly in your mind. Perform the Banishing Ritual of the Middle Finger and bellow the following space claiming formula at the image:

"This is my fucking exercise and I don't give a good God Damn what you think of it!" Clearly see the image of your critic dissolve into a little pool of slime to be washed away by a gentle rain (or monsoon.) Treat yourself to something fun when you are finished. Never read a dead wood essay critically. If it exists, it's perfect.

PHASE II—STEP I

Cutting Kindling

If you are lucky enough to live in an industrialized nation, you are probably 15 minutes away from a library with a reference section. A moderately intelligent person with some effort and a reference library could take over the world, start a new religion, end world hunger, change the flashing 12:00 on the VCR... When you get free power, use it.

Select the five most interesting words—your choice, there are no wrong answers—from your dead wood pile and list them in your journal. These are the big branches that need to be chopped into kindling. Give each word a page to itself. The reference librarian will be happy to show you the Unabridged Dictionary, the Dictionary of Word Histories (also called the Dictionary of Etymology), and Roget's International Thesaurus.

By hand, copy the entire listing for your words out of an Unabridged Dictionary and the Dictionary of Etymology. Select some words that look neat out of the Thesaurus's listing, and look them up. Satisfactory completion of the

exercise demands only two copied listings for each of your
five words.

PHASE II—STEP II

Photocopy your journal pages (maximum of eight, including your word research.) Cut up the pages so that there are
very few, if any, complete sentences, but lots and lots of
word groups. Don't worry about cutting words in half; you
are allowed to make up new words whenever you want.
Select from the kindling at random, and tape together a
resulting page or two. Copy it into your journal and underline the parts which tickle you, or which seem particularly
strange and interesting. This method has been adapted from
the works of William S. Burroughs and Brion Gysin.
Advanced students should check out their other methods
for empowering the creative response.

Advanced Exercises

a) Select five reference volumes at random, or five that
are unfamiliar to you. By any means necessary, relate your
words and ideas from a dead wood paper to the subject
matter covered in the reference volume. Look up the results
and put any interesting correspondences or new information
that you find into your journal. Resist the temptation to
believe that aliens are communicating with you. Any two
ideas can be related, so look for unusually elegant or clever
relations.

b) Go to a University library and venture into the section
where the research journals are kept. These are highly spe-
cialized and difficult volumes full of neat information.
Don't worry about whether or not you understand what you
read. Learn to tolerate ambiguity and frustration. Delve into
arcane branches of physics, mathematics, and linguistics.
Jot down anything interesting that you find. Try to look up
words, symbols, and ideas that you don't understand. Let
the natural explorer inside you come alive.

Resolve to explore a minimum of ten new journals or reference volumes a month. Beware ye unwary practitioners of this most deadly and dangerous magic! An infinite universe is opening before you!

PHASE III

Lighting the Fire

Enter stage left, the first sustained effort on the part of the creative identity:

Write a poem, to the best of your ability, based solely on your cut-up exercise. Remember not to expect too much or to be too hard on yourself. Piling too much wood on a tiny flame will only quench it. Do your best with your understanding of rhythm, analogy, sound, allusion, etc. It is important that you try your best; it is not important that your critical self approve of your results. Revise your first attempt a couple of times. Utilize your new research skills to add complexity in moderate doses. When you finish the first edition of one poem, start four more simultaneously. Use your dead wood pile, your kindling pile, your random wandering through the research bins. Photocopy it all and cut it up if you wish, but don't rely solely on random forces for your poems, not for this exercise anyway.

When you have five poems, title them by opening books randomly until you find a phrase that you like. These poems are going to be magical formulae which you will utilize for one of the most feared and powerful rituals in the arsenal of a magician: "Prophesying from the Mouths of the Dead." Correct the poem's spelling, adjust wording which you find awkward, admire the results of your labor, and type the finally completed form.

Advanced Exercises

a) Purchase a good rhyming dictionary that contains a section dedicated to poetic forms (i.e., sonnets, haiku, elegies etc.) Try to write a poem that fits the forms. Don't worry about the quality or inspiration at first. People who invoke these considerations too much before settling down to work are just looking for a reason to cop out. Always put the latest edition of whichever poem you are working with in your journal.

b) Try to rewrite conversations you had during the day. Don't worry about relevance; shoot for accuracy. Once you have about ten short conversations in your journal, pick any two at random and attempt to combine them. Work over your conversations in terms of what you wish you had said, in terms of what you wish the other had said.

PHASE IV

Prophesying From The Mouths Of The Dead

The creative fire of a magician has the most amazing effect on the uncreative dead. While normally these impotent souls wander the face of the earth producing and consuming, contributing nothing of themselves, when they behold the creative fire, they speak!

"That's not art!" (in a groaning whining voice)

"That's immoral!"

"That's not good enough!"

As magicians, we recognize this inevitable phenomenon as neither good nor evil and concern ourselves only with how we can take advantage of it. This exercise, which transforms the inane babbling of the world's wraiths and zombies into still further creation is called "Prophesying from the mouths of the Dead."

Most people have pretty firm ideas about things, which they have picked up here and there, like social diseases. A frightening number of these people go so far as to believe that they are right! Some even think that their ideas are God's ideas, still others that they have the only ideas. Hopefully you can find five people who have been told by God that they are Right. These people are a wonderful resource, in that they act as channels to other more creative people (saints, prophets, priests, talk show hosts…) By learning the One True Doctrine, they eliminate the need to struggle with uncertainty which is faced by the rest of us mere humans. They surrender the creative identity and their right to be wrong, and so become vehicles for the One True Doctrine.

Take your five channels and tell them (one at a time) that you are doing an exercise for a writing class, and that you want their help in interpreting a poem you have culled from a contemporary literature journal. Do not tell them that they are reading your poem. Tape-record the session, with their permission. Ask them questions about poetry in general.

When you are done, transcribe the interesting parts of the interview into your journal. This part of the exercise is very important. It shows how to creatively interpret input from non-creative sources, and direct its energy in creative directions. This transformation of twaddle into art, under the direction of the creative identity, is the key to living free in a hateful and hostile world.

Take your five "essays" and from them playfully derive rules for the criticism of poetry. From a combination of all five recordings, derive a single passionate (if self-contradictory and absurd) theory of literary criticism. Include general rules that your zombies hinted at, any strong opinions that they actually expressed, biases that are obvious from their emotional reactions, or the lack thereof. Give yourself a few days with this exercise. Have fun with it. Don't consciously mock your critics—develop with all possible sincerity the Only Right Method for interpreting poetry. Correct the spelling on the final edition. Type one copy as if for publication in a literary journal, and place one copy in your own journal.

Advanced Exercises

Play the same game as you did with poetry interpretation with sex, politics, religion, contemporary issues, and so forth. Collect the most vehement and absurd opinions in your journal. The best results come from truly pompous and self-righteous people. Synthesize widely varying but equally emotionally intense positions into opinion papers or political platforms for non-existent parties, try to publish these as letters to the editor in the local papers.

PHASE V

Cooking Your Food and Keeping Warm— Publish or Perish?

Don't get all caught up in this part of the exercise. It is better that you do it poorly and get it done, than not to do it at all by making too much of it. The goal is not to actually publish something per se, but merely to get over the fear of submitting your work (there are analogies beyond writing here.) Learn to deal with being an object for someone else's criticism. Learn to stand naked!

Find a journal of contemporary poetry at your local university library or the closest thing to which you have access. Select an interesting poem, and analyze it according to the theory which you made up in the previous section. Write up your analysis, couple it with a statement of your theory, and send it to the literary journal. It doesn't matter which one. Demand $500 for the right to publish your work. Send your five poems to another journal, demand $50 apiece for them. You may wish to do this under a pen name. When the responses come, tape them into your journal, cut up photocopies of them into your poems, and congratulate yourself on being one of the few with the guts and the energy to see through a difficult project to its completion. The world is filled with people who cut themselves off unnecessarily from the bounty of information and opportunity which surrounds them. Overcome restriction.

Now, you decide what you accomplished, if anything. Write me with your success stories!

THE MAGIC PILL OF ENLIGHTENMENT

BY JOHN DEMMITT

Dr. Hyatt has said in several of his works that the Law of the New Aeon is *DO IT*. I am well aware of the fact that 95% (Am I being generous?) of the people who read this book will not even take the time to go through the aphorisms even once, let alone perform the entire operation. It is sad, considering that this is one of the simpler exercises capable of creating real change. My assumption makes me wonder how many of the 5% who do the exercises will then go on to other, more difficult, practices.

My message is simple: *THERE ARE NO MAGIC PILLS!* Anyone or anything that claims to be an easy way or an easy path is just a way of catering to your Zombie self. In reality, these types of methods will only succeed in putting you further and further into hypnosis. Just reading this book can only take you so far. The rest of the way requires hard work and dedication. Not dedication to some group, idea, or system, but dedication to yourself. Strangely, most people find this hard to do.

The thought of a magic pill reminds me of the alchemists of old (and new) who were seeking the elixir of life. For most of them, this work was in vain. But a very few of them actually were willing to dedicate themselves to good, practical work, and were able to achieve some change in their character structure. Immortality is another story. But science has shown us that immortality is a simple biochemical problem (even if they seem unwilling to solve it). Personal change is not so simple, however.

It is understandable that most people are looking for this magic pill, especially in America. In this age of science, we have learned that when you have a cold, you go to the drug store and get some medicine. Virus? Penicillin. Flu? Go get a shot. So what if it doesn't work? Many forms of human misery and suffering are alleviated this way. Feeling depressed? Go see a shrink, a psychic, a priest, or better yet, take some valium, prozac, lithium. The shrink, the psychic and the priest will patch you up enough to face a little more upset, and the valium will make you feel nothing at all.

Most will admit that these are only temporary solutions—as they swallow that pill—and most will realize that it takes many years to actually achieve something with the shrink. I ask, however, achieve what? Only a deeper hypnosis, in most cases. Anyone who actually examines the role of so-called therapy today, and the so-called theories that they are based on, will see that the disease is being *not normal*—i.e., being other than what every Moolah thinks you should be like—and the cure is to suppress those "antisocial" urges. But who is to say that the middle-class has any idea of what is normal, when they are all experiencing depression, anxiety, anger, and fear most of their lives?

This illusion of normality is based upon an idea that is worshipped as a god. It is the TV-Hollywood 1950's family, where everyone is happy, where problems get resolved in a half hour, where everything stays constantly the same. Well, guess what? It is no longer the 50's. It is the 1990's, and not only does that reality not exist anymore, it died because it failed. The violence, crime, addiction, mental "disease," suicide, child abuse, rape, etc. that we hear (and maybe see) so much is a more accurate reflection of human normality than the *Leave It To Beaver* model. The problem is that few people want to recognize anxiety, fear and anger as being *normal*, and therefore don't recognize that the violent outward expressions are just a reaction against the attempt to repress normal feelings.

So the vicious cycle begins. Fears are created about being afraid. Which of course leads to other symptoms which "society" views as "abnormal." So what does society try to cure? Not the repression of the natural fear, violence, and anxiety which causes this behavior, but the fear, violence, and anxiety itself. In other words, they attempt to repress it more. And once again, the cycle continues, until we have created a "society" where everyone lives in fear, and in fear of fear, and in fear of violence, and react violently against the fear of violence, and are afraid of their reactions. And why so much fear? Because they believe that it is not "normal," and being "abnormal" is very "bad."

It seems that this notion of what is "normal" is based upon ideas about what a highly evolved and rational race should be. Now this is based upon two fallacies: firstly, that humans are highly evolved, and secondly, that they are rational. So if the premise is wrong, might also be the conclusion? Our "irrational" natures are not supposed to be there. But the fact is that they are. So if fear, violence, anxiety, etc. are *natural*, and not symptoms of abnormal function, is it not "rational" to believe that these ideas of how a rational race should behave are irrational?

Now the question remains, what can we do to get back in touch with our "natural" selves? The key word in this sentence is DO. It took a very few years in childhood to create this fear of being yourself, and the rest of your life has been spent reinforcing those fears. No magic pill is going to cure this. No book is going to cure this. Only good, hard work, and lots of time.

Part of the problem is that there are so many "solutions" out there for one to choose from. How is one to know what is good and what is bad. Well firstly, you will never know if you just keep looking and never doing. But what to do? If it's easy, if it makes you feel "good," then it is probably just putting you back to sleep. If it actually requires you to put forth effort, if it makes you feel both "good" and "bad," then maybe you have found something.

If you have ever read any of Dr. Hyatt's other works, you have been lucky enough to stumble upon some of the methods that can accomplish this "cure." Chances are, however, that even with this lucky opportunity, you have not taken advantage of it. But if you are really interested in change, and not just some reading material to use as pornography for your mental masturbation, then *DO IT!* There are other methods, other practices, but not one of them will be found to be easy. You must first overcome the fear of starting (overcome, not repress), and then you must overcome the fears, anxieties, and other "negative" feelings that you will experience and re-experience as you do the work. So many excuses not to continue, and only one good reason to go on: real change.

If you have not read Dr. Hyatt's other works, and you are interested in real change, you can start with *Undoing Yourself*. Then again, if you are not interested in real change, Dr. Hyatt's other books are also excellent pornography for mental masturbation.

Either way, have you done the exercises in this book? Start there, and you may just overcome that fear of starting something new. Maybe it will be easier for you to go on to other work. Probably not, but it can't hurt. Or can it?

CATEGORICAL IMPERATORS

ILLUSTRATED BY S. JASON BLACK

The Staff of New Falcon Publications

Dr. Hyatt Guarding His Eggs

Einstein After Relativity

The First Safe Cracker

Jung Discovering the Archetypes

Pre-Sex–Transplant Victim

The First Feet-al Transplant
(Not A Bush Supporter)

Dr. Hyatt Receives His Royalty Check